CYRUS ELLISON

# GOD'S GAME CHANGERS

**40 Faith Fueled Inspirational Sports Stories for Teens to Build Unshakable Confidence, Crush Goals, and Forge Exceptional Character**

# FROM: _______________

# TO: _______________

# DATE: _______________

# NOTE: _______________

# TABLE OF CONTENTS



## 1: IDENTITY — YOU BEFORE THE UNIFORM



## 2: DISCIPLINE — THE GRIND NOBODY SEES



## 3: CONFIDENCE — SILENCING "YOU CAN'T"

YOU CAN'T

# PRAISE

**Jordan W., 9th Grader and Girls Varsity Track Athlete**

"I almost didn't read God's Game Changers. I assumed it would just say pray more and try harder. It's nothing like that. The Sydney McLaughlin-Levrone chapter on competing for an Audience of One changed my race-day mindset. I used to feel like I would throw up before every 400. My coach kept saying relax, but no one showed me how. Reading how Sydney stopped chasing approval and anchored herself in Colossians 3:23-24 gave me something practical. Before every race now, I remind myself I'm running for God and the pressure drops. My times improved, but the biggest change is I stopped comparing myself to the girl in the next lane. The Allyson Felix story also hit hard. A growth spurt messed up my mechanics and I felt like my body was betraying me. This book taught me real mental armor is knowing who you are in Christ before the starter pistol goes off. The reflections made it stick because I was applying what I read. Every athlete I know needs this."

**David and Karen L., Parents of a 16 Year Old Football Player**

*"Our son was in the worst mental place of his athletic life after being moved to second string. He kept saying I'm not good enough and maybe football isn't for me. We gave him God's Game Changers without expecting much. He read four chapters the first night. The Jalen Hurts chapter rewired everything. Seeing how Hurts lost his starting job and leaned on Psalm 56:3 showed our son that being benched is not the end. It can be preparation. The next week at practice his coach said he looked like a different kid. The Tim Tebow chapter sparked an hour-long family conversation about courage and conviction. Now our son does the reflections every Sunday and we talk through them together. This book gave him mental armor and gave us our kid back. If your teen is struggling with confidence or identity, this is the book that breaks through."*

**Aaliyah R., High School Senior & Club Volleyball Player**

*"The Simone Biles chapter made me cry. Seeing the greatest gymnast*

*rely on faith under world-level pressure yet still declare her worth beyond results showed me what I needed to see. I've struggled with anxiety since freshman year. It got so bad I would freeze in crucial sets. The Coco Gauff chapter described exactly what I feel carrying everyone's expectations. She cast her anxiety on God through 1 Peter 5:7 and that verse is now written on my knee pad. This book taught me real mental armor is not pretending pressure isn't there. It's knowing God is bigger than it. The reflections forced me to write what I believe and live it. I bought copies for teammates and we text our reflections weekly. This book is why I'm playing with joy again."*

**Pastor Terrance J., Youth Minister & Baseball Chaplain**

*"Finally, a resource that connects Scripture and competition so athletes listen, engage deeply, and build real mental armor."*

**Lisa M., Mother of a 13-Year-Old Gymnast**

*"My daughter started gymnastics at five. By twelve she was burned out and terrified of competing. She shook during warmups and begged to skip meets. Then we found God's Game Changers. The Simone Biles chapter changed everything. My daughter said if the greatest gymnast ever feels this pressure and still turns to God, maybe I'm not broken. That sentence alone was worth the book many times over. The Gabby Douglas story also hit deeply. Girls at her gym mocked her body and those voices became her inner voice. Seeing Gabby hold Isaiah 54:17 taught her those words don't define her. She began doing the reflections nightly and finally processed fears instead of burying them. Her coach recently said she looks calm on beam in a way she never has. This book gave my daughter mental armor and gave her back the joy gymnastics had stolen."*

**Coach DeAndre H., Varsity Basketball Coach & Athletic Director**

*"In twenty years of coaching, this is the first sports mindset book my players actually read and apply. It grounds identity in Christ, dismantles comparison and doubt, and transforms team culture. Our athletes now engage eagerly in reflection and Scripture. I'm ordering copies for our entire athletic program."*

# PRE-GAME

January 2, 2023. Monday Night Football. Millions of people watch as Buffalo Bills safety Damar Hamlin makes a routine tackle, stands up, and collapses. His heart stops on national television. Players from both teams fall to their knees and cry. An entire nation begins to pray. Days later, Damar opens his eyes. His first words of gratitude go straight to God. Months later, he plays football again. The doctors called it a medical miracle. Damar called it faith.

That moment revealed a truth the sports world rarely talks about. When the stats, the trophies, and the spotlight get stripped away, the only thing left standing is what you truly believe. And that belief can change everything.

This is a book about 40 athletes who proved it.

You are about to walk with Tim Tebow as millions mock him for praying on national television and he refuses to flinch. You will stand with Simone Biles on the Olympic floor in the most terrifying moment of her career and discover why walking away took more courage than any gold medal. You will watch Michael Jordan get cut from his high school basketball team and learn the Christ-shaped mindset that turned rejection into the greatest legacy in sports history. You will run alongside Giannis Antetokounmpo as he goes from selling sunglasses on the streets of Athens to holding the NBA MVP trophy with tears streaming down his face. You will sit with Kobe Bryant in an empty gym at 4 AM and understand why his relentless discipline was an offering, not an obsession. You will meet Serena Williams, Patrick Mahomes, Coco Gauff, Kevin Durant, Sydney McLaughlin-Levrone, Russell Wilson, Clayton Kershaw, Abby Wambach, Katie Ledecky, and dozens more, every one of them a follower of Jesus who faced a Christ-centered turning point that redefined their purpose far beyond the scoreboard.

But here is why this book was written for you specifically.

Maybe you are the kid stuck on the bench wondering if the coach even sees you. Maybe you are the starter who looks confident but secretly feels like a fraud. Maybe your worst game is still replaying in your head on an endless loop. Maybe your team culture is toxic.

Maybe the pressure from parents, social media, or your own expectations has made your sport stop feeling fun. Maybe you quietly wonder if God cares about any of this.

He does. And every story in this book will prove it.

Each chapter gives you a Christ-anchored Scripture, a vivid real-life athlete story, a personal reflection question, a short prayer, and one specific practice step you can act on today. Not someday. Today. The chapters are short enough to read in five minutes and powerful enough to shift your entire mindset before a game, a practice, or a hard conversation. You can read one story a day as a devotional. You can binge it on a road trip. You can flip straight to the chapter that matches whatever you are facing right now. Seven chapters cover confidence, discipline, resilience, mental toughness, comeback, leadership, and legacy, and every single one maps directly to the real battles you are already fighting.

This is not a lecture. It is not a guilt trip. It is a Christ-fueled playbook built to help you build unshakable confidence, crush your goals, and forge the kind of character that lasts long after your final whistle blows.

Forty athletes. Forty Scriptures. Forty breakthroughs that will change the way you see your sport, your struggles, and your God.

Turn the page. Your game is about to change.

# HOW TO USE THIS BOOK

This book was built to fit your life, not the other way around. There is no right or wrong way to read it. Here are a few simple ways to get the most out of every page.

One Story A Day. Read one chapter each morning or night like a devotional. Let the Scripture sink in. Answer the reflection question honestly. Pray the prayer. Do the practice step. In 40 days, you will have walked through every lesson in this book and built habits that stick.

Flip to What You Need. Having a tough week with confidence? Open Chapter One. Recovering from an injury or a painful loss? Jump straight to Chapter Five. You do not have to read this in order. Let your current struggle guide you to the story that speaks loudest.

Read It With Someone. Grab a parent, a sibling, a teammate, or a friend. Read one story out loud together and talk through the reflection question. Some of the best conversations you will ever have with the people you love will start inside these pages.

Bring It to Your Team. Coaches, captains, and team leaders, use one chapter a week for team devotionals, pre-game talks, or locker room culture sessions. The stories are short enough to read in five minutes and powerful enough to shift the entire energy of your squad.

Use It in Youth Group or Bible Study. Each chapter pairs a Scripture with a real-life athlete story, a reflection question, a prayer, and a practice step. That is a ready-made small group session with zero extra prep.

Gift It Forward. When a chapter hits you in the chest, do not keep it to yourself. Hand this book to the teammate who is struggling, the friend who just got cut, or the younger athlete who looks up to you. One story shared at the right moment can change someone's entire trajectory. Buy an extra copy. Leave it in the locker room. Pass it around the bus. Let it spread.

Pair It With the Accountability Calendar. To keep your momentum going long after you finish reading, use the companion Advent-style accountability calendar designed to walk you through daily action steps that match the lessons in this book.

No pressure. No guilt. No perfect way to do this. Just start.

Stop navigating the high-pressure, toxic sports and school culture alone.

Join a our community of Christian parents dedicated to building rooted reens who are even stronger in their faith.

What's Inside the Community:

» Safe Community: Connect with parents who value character over the scoreboard.

» Use the map to connect to other Christian parents close to you who also bought our books and joined.

» Get all of our next books sent to you for free as an advanced reviewer.

» Custom Worship Song: A professional anthem featuring your teens name & scripture of your choice ($250 Value!)

» Recruiting & Scholarship Kit: Clear steps to the next level without the stress.

» More bonuses and materials added continously!

Scan the QR code to Join us.

# 1: IDENTITY — YOU BEFORE THE UNIFORM

# 01

# TIM TEBOW: BEYOND THE HIGHLIGHTS

"For you created my inmost being; you knit me together in my mother's womb. I praise you because I am fearfully and wonderfully made." — Psalm 139:13-14

Tim Tebow stands on stage in New York City, gripping the Heisman Trophy with both hands. The audience erupts. Camera flashes explode like lightning across the ballroom. The University of Florida quarterback just became the first sophomore in history to win college football's highest individual honor. His name is everywhere. His jersey is the top seller in America. On national television, he drops to one knee and thanks God, a moment so iconic that "Tebowing" becomes a word people use around the world.

But fast forward a few years, and the cheering stops. Tim gets drafted by the Denver Broncos and leads a miraculous playoff run, but then he gets traded. Then benched. Then cut. Then cut again. Team after team decides he is not their guy. The same sports channels that celebrated him now run segments asking if his career is finished. Social media fills with jokes. The highlight reel that once defined him starts to feel like ancient history.

Here is where most people would crumble. But Tim never crumbled because Tim never built his identity on football in the first place. He built it on Psalm 139:13-14. He believed deep in his bones that God crafted him on purpose and with purpose. Football was something he did. It was never who he was. When the NFL said "you are not enough," Tim already had his answer: "God says I am fearfully and wonderfully made, and that settles it."

After football, Tim played professional baseball, launched a foundation that has served thousands of people with special needs, became a bestselling author, and inspired millions through speaking. He did not shrink when his highlight reel stopped playing. He expanded into everything God had waiting for him.

Now think about your life. Maybe your whole friend group knows you as "the soccer kid" or "the swimmer." Maybe when your sport goes well, you feel amazing, and when it goes badly, you feel worthless. That is a dangerous ride because seasons end, injuries happen, and coaches change their minds. But your identity in Christ never changes. You were handcrafted by God before you ever touched a ball, a bat, or a track. Your worth was decided before your first game.

You are not your highlight reel. You are His masterpiece. Let that truth be the foundation everything else stands on.

## Reflection:

Tim Tebow lost his NFL career but never lost himself because his identity was built on God, not football. Your sport is something you do, not someone you are. What would you be if your sport disappeared tomorrow?

## Prayer:

God, remind me daily that my identity lives in You, not my performance. I am Yours completely. Amen.

## Practice:

Write "I am God's masterpiece" on your mirror. Read it before every practice and game this week.

# 02

# SIMONE BILES: HEART OVER MEDALS

"The Lord does not look at the things people look at. People look at the outward appearance, but the Lord looks at the heart." — 1 Samuel 16:7

Simone Biles launches off the vault at the 2016 Rio Olympics and soars through the air like gravity simply forgot about her. She sticks the landing with barely a wobble. The judges flash their scores and the arena explodes. Gold medal. Then another. And another. And another. Four gold medals in a single Olympics. The world calls her the greatest gymnast who ever lived. Her smile lights up every magazine cover on the planet. From the outside, Simone Biles has everything completely figured out.

Then comes Tokyo 2021. The biggest stage in the world. Billions of people watching. And in the middle of competition, Simone does something nobody expected. She withdraws. Not because of a broken ankle or a torn muscle. She steps back because her mind and heart are screaming for help. The pressure of being perfect has become a weight too heavy for even the strongest gymnast in history to carry. Some people praise her courage. Others call her a quitter. The opinions fly in from every direction like dodgeballs she cannot duck.

But Simone had been growin

g in her faith through all of it. She leaned into a truth that most champions take years to discover: God does not measure her worth by the scoreboard. First Samuel 16:7 says people judge by what they see on the outside, but God looks straight at the heart. Simone realized that if her value depended on gold medals, she would spend her whole life terrified of the day she stopped winning. That is a prison, not a podium.

Think about how this hits your life right now. Maybe you had a terrible game last weekend and you felt like a completely different person on Monday morning. Maybe you only feel confident when your stats look good. That means you have handed your value over to a scoreboard, and scoreboards change every single game. God's love for you does not rise and fall with your batting average or your free throw percentage. He is not checking the leaderboard to decide if you matter.

You are more than your greatest win and more than your worst loss. When you let God define your value instead of your results, you compete with freedom instead of fear. That is where real greatness begins.

## Reflection:

Simone Biles walked away from Olympic gold to protect her heart because she knew God's love is not earned through medals. Your worst game does not shrink your worth. When did you last tie your value to a result?

## Prayer:

Father, free me from measuring my worth by results. Teach me to see myself through Your loving eyes. Amen.

## Practice:

After your next game, write one thing you loved about competing that has nothing to do with the score.

# 03

# SYDNEY MCLAUGHLIN: AUDIENCE OF ONE

"Whatever you do, work at it with all your heart, as working for the Lord, not for human masters, since you know that you will receive an inheritance from the Lord as a reward." — Colossians 3:23-24

Sydney McLaughlin-Levrone crosses the finish line at the 2022 World Championships and the clock flashes a number that makes the entire stadium hold its breath. Another world record in the 400-meter hurdles. She pulls away from her competitors like they are standing still. The crowd in Eugene, Oregon, rises to their feet. Commentators stumble over their words trying to describe what they just witnessed. But instead of pumping her fists or pointing at the scoreboard, Sydney closes her eyes, presses her hands together, and whispers a prayer right there on the track. She is not performing for the cameras. She is thanking the only audience that matters to her.

Sydney grew up in New Jersey as a track prodigy. By sixteen she was competing at the Olympics. The attention was enormous. Sponsorship deals, social media followers, and constant pressure to prove she deserved the hype. She admits that for years she chased the approval of coaches, fans, and commentators. Every race felt like a test she could not afford to fail. The anxiety was suffocating. She was winning medals but losing her peace.

Everything shifted when Sydney deepened her relationship with Jesus. She discovered Colossians 3:23-24 and it rewired her entire approach. She stopped running to impress people and started running as worship. She shared publicly that her purpose is not to collect trophies but to glorify God with the legs He gave her. When she runs for an audience of One, the opinions of thousands lose their grip on her heart.

This is huge for you. Maybe you replay your coach's criticism on repeat inside your head at night. Maybe you check how many likes your game highlights get and feel crushed when the number is low. Craving approval from every direction will drain you completely dry. But when you decide that God is your primary audience, something incredible happens. You still compete hard. You still chase excellence. But the fear of disappointing people stops controlling your every move.

Run your race, play your game, and give your absolute best. But do it for Him. When His opinion is the one you care about most, pressure transforms into pure purpose. That is freedom no trophy can ever give you.

## Reflection:

Sydney McLaughlin-Levrone broke world records in track by running for God instead of chasing human approval. Freedom came when she stopped performing for the crowd. Whose opinion controls how you feel about yourself after a competition?

## Prayer:

Lord, I choose to perform for You alone. Free me from the exhausting trap of people's approval today. Amen.

## Practice:

Before your next competition, whisper "This is for You, God." Notice how it changes the way you compete.

# 04

# JONATHAN ISAAC: STANDING FOR FAITH

"Do not conform to the pattern of this world, but be transformed by the renewing of your mind." — Romans 12:2

Jonathan Isaac stands at center court in the NBA bubble in Orlando as the national anthem begins to play. Every single player and coach around him kneels. The cameras sweep across the arena capturing a sea of bent knees. And then they find Jonathan. He is the only one standing. Six feet eleven inches tall, hands clasped together, eyes steady, standing completely alone in front of millions of viewers around the world. The internet erupts within seconds. His name trends on every social media platform. Some people call him brave. Others attack him with vicious comments. He simply calls himself faithful.

Jonathan is a forward for the Orlando Magic who grew up in a Christian home and gave his life to Jesus at a young age. When the intense social pressure of 2020 swept through professional sports, Jonathan had a clear choice. He could follow the crowd and avoid controversy, or he could follow his convictions and face the firestorm. He chose his faith. In interviews after that moment, Jonathan pointed straight to Romans 12:2. He explained that God calls us not to blend into the world's mold but to be transformed from the inside out. He was not making a political statement. He was making a faith statement.

What most people did not see was how hard that moment truly was. Jonathan later shared that his hands were trembling. Standing alone is never comfortable. But he discovered that God does not call us to be comfortable. He calls us to be courageous. Jonathan also faced a devastating knee injury that same season, and his faith carried him through months of painful rehabilitation. His identity was not shaken because it was anchored in something far deeper than basketball or public opinion.

Now bring this into your world. Maybe your teammates pressure you to skip church for extra hangouts. Maybe your friends mock prayer or roll their eyes when you mention God. It feels so much easier to stay quiet, to laugh along, to disappear into the crowd. But Romans 12:2 is an invitation to stand tall even when standing means standing by yourself. You do not need the crowd's permission to follow Jesus.

Every time you choose faith over fitting in, your character grows stronger. You become someone others can trust deeply. You become a leader worth following. Stand tall today. God is standing right beside you.

---

## Reflection:

Jonathan Isaac stood alone in front of millions because his faith was louder than his fear. Courage is not the absence of trembling. It is choosing God anyway. Where in your life are you hiding your faith to fit in?

---

## Prayer:

Jesus, give me courage to stand for You even when I stand alone. Strengthen my heart right now. Amen.

---

## Practice:

This week, share one thing you believe with someone even if it feels uncomfortable. Notice God's strength show up.

# 05

# KEVIN DURANT: THE REAL MVP

"Start children off on the way they should go, and even when they are old they will not turn from it." — Proverbs 22:6

Kevin Durant steps to the podium to accept the NBA's Most Valuable Player award. The basketball world expects the usual polished thank-yous to coaches and teammates. But Kevin's voice cracks instantly. Tears flood his eyes. He looks directly at his mother Wanda sitting in the front row and says four words that shake the entire room: "You the real MVP." The toughest player in the arena is sobbing like a child because the woman who built his soul is watching her seed finally bloom. The whole audience weeps with him.

Growing up in Prince George's County, Maryland, Kevin and his family moved from apartment to apartment constantly. Money was painfully tight. Stability felt like a luxury they simply could not afford. But Wanda Pratt made one thing absolutely non-negotiable: faith. She took Kevin and his brother to church every Sunday. She prayed over them before school. She posted Bible verses on the refrigerator door. Some mornings there was barely enough food on the table, but there was always enough Scripture in the house. Wanda was planting Proverbs 22:6 into her boys without ever quoting the chapter and verse. She was training them in the way they should go, trusting that God would hold them steady when life felt shaky and uncertain.

Kevin carried that foundation all the way to the peak of professional basketball. Through every championship run and every setback, he credits his mother's faithful prayers as the bedrock beneath his feet.

Now here is the honest part. Maybe your home looks nothing like Kevin's. Maybe nobody in your house reads the Bible or prays before dinner. Maybe faith feels like something other families have and you are building from the ground up all alone. Hear this clearly: God is not limited by your address or your family situation. He can build a foundation in your heart through a coach who believes in you, a mentor at youth group, a teammate who prays, or even through this chapter you are reading right now. Proverbs 22:6 is not just for parents. It is God's promise that seeds planted early grow roots that last a lifetime.

If you have someone pouring faith into your life, thank them today. If you do not have that person yet, ask God to send them. He is faithful and always building something beautiful.

## Reflection:

Kevin Durant credited his mother Wanda for building his foundation through prayer and faithfulness during the hardest seasons. Faith roots can be planted by anyone God sends your way. Who is pouring into your faith right now?

## Prayer:

God, thank You for every person who plants faith in me. Build my foundation strong even from scratch. Amen.

## Practice:

Text or thank one person who has encouraged your faith this week. If no one comes to mind, ask God to send someone.

# 06

# SERENA WILLIAMS: BREAKING EVERY MOLD

"'For I know the plans I have for you,' declares the Lord, 'plans to prosper you and not to harm you, plans to give you hope and a future.'" — Jeremiah 29:11

Serena Williams lifts the Australian Open trophy high above her head in January 2017, and the crowd inside Rod Laver Arena roars with pure admiration. She has just won her twenty-third Grand Slam singles title, the most in the modern era of tennis. She is the undisputed greatest to ever grip a racket. But the world almost never got to witness a single moment of it.

Rewind to Compton, California, in the early 1990s. Two young Black girls are hitting tennis balls on cracked public courts littered with broken glass. Gunshots occasionally echo in the distance. Their father Richard holds a handwritten plan, dozens of pages long, that he created before either daughter was even born. The tennis world looks at the Williams family and laughs out loud. Tennis is a country club sport dominated by wealthy families with private coaching. Nobody from Compton is supposed to play this game, let alone dominate it. Coaches whisper that Serena is too muscular, too aggressive, too different. Tournament officials question her clothing, her intensity, and her confidence. Every single step of the way, someone is holding up a mold and telling Serena she does not fit inside it.

But Serena held tight to a belief that God's plan for her life was bigger than any box humans could build. Jeremiah 29:11 was not just a verse on a page. It was the blueprint she trusted when the world tried to shrink her down to size. God declared He had plans to prosper her, and she took Him at His word. Every championship she won was proof that God's design cannot be contained by human limitations.

Now think about the labels people have stuck on you. Too loud. Too quiet. Too tall. Too short. Too emotional. Too intense. Those labels are just molds that other people constructed, and you were never designed to squeeze yourself inside them. God built you with specific gifts, a specific fire, and a specific purpose that no human category can contain.

When someone tells you that you do not fit, smile and remember this: you were never supposed to. God did not create you to blend into someone else's blueprint. He created you to shatter it and walk boldly into the future He already planned just for you. The mold is broken. Your purpose is wide open.

---

## Reflection:

---

Serena Williams shattered every mold tennis tried to force her into because she trusted God's plan over people's opinions. Labels only stick if you let them. What limiting label are you carrying that God never gave you?

---

## Prayer:

---

Lord, I reject every mold the world built for me. I trust Your plans are bigger and better. Amen.

---

## Practice:

---

Write down one limiting label someone gave you. Cross it out and write God's truth over it right now.

# 2: DISCIPLINE — THE GRIND NOBODY SEES

# 07

# KOBE BRYANT: THE 4AM ADVANTAGE

"Diligent hands will rule, but laziness ends in forced labor." - Proverbs 12:24

Kobe Bryant, the legendary basketball icon who wore the Los Angeles Lakers purple and gold for twenty electrifying seasons, once asked a trainer a simple question that changed everything. "Have you ever seen 4 AM in Los Angeles?" The trainer shook his head. Kobe smiled. He had seen it thousands of times. While the city slept beneath a blanket of fog and dim streetlights, Kobe was already in the gym. The squeak of his sneakers echoed through an empty practice facility. No teammates. No coaches yelling plays. Just Kobe, a rack of basketballs, and a frightening hunger to improve.

His routine was legendary. He would rise at 4 AM, complete a full workout before most people touched their alarm clocks, then show up to team practice looking fresh. His teammates would arrive and find him already drenched in sweat, having made 800 shots before they even stretched. People called it "Mamba Mentality," but at its root it was something far deeper. It was Proverbs 12:24 made real. Diligent hands will rule. Not talented hands. Not lucky hands. Diligent ones. Kobe understood that the early hours belonged to the hungry, and the hungry eventually become the ones who lead.

Kobe grew up in a Catholic household and carried a deep reverence for discipline that went beyond basketball. He believed God handed him a gift, and wasting that gift by sleeping in would be an insult to the Giver. His dark morning sessions were an offering of obedience. Every shot made before sunrise was a thank you note written in sweat.

For you as a teen athlete, this hits close to home. You know the feeling of grinding hard only when a big game is coming or when a coach is watching. But what about Tuesday morning when nobody cares? What about the offseason when your friends are playing video games? The 4 AM advantage is not really about waking before dawn. It is about choosing effort when there is zero applause. It means doing your stretches alone in your room. It means studying film on your phone during lunch. It means praying for strength before your feet even touch the floor.

The world will only ever see your highlight reel. But God sees your 4 AM. He sees the work nobody claps for. And that quiet, faithful work is exactly what builds champions.

## Reflection:

Kobe Bryant proved that diligent, unseen effort separates great athletes from average ones. Talent alone is never enough without relentless daily discipline. When no one is watching, do you still give your absolute best? What is one area where you can start working harder in silence?

## Prayer:

Lord, give me strength to work when no one watches. Let my hidden discipline honor the gifts You placed inside me. Amen.

## Practice:

Tomorrow, wake thirty minutes earlier. Train, stretch, or pray before anyone else rises. Notice how it changes your day.

# 08

# KATIE LEDECKY: BORING IS BEAUTIFUL

"Let us not become weary in doing good, for at the proper time we will reap a harvest if we do not give up." - Galatians 6:9

The pool looks the same every single morning. Same blue tiles. Same black lane lines stretching endlessly forward. Same sharp smell of chlorine hanging thick in the humid air. For Katie Ledecky, the dominant force in distance swimming and one of the most decorated Olympic swimmers in history, this sameness is the whole point. While other athletes chase highlight moments, Katie quietly chases the clock, one identical lap at a time.

At the 2016 Rio Olympics, Katie touched the wall in the 800 meter freestyle a full eleven seconds ahead of the silver medalist. Eleven seconds in swimming is an ocean. The crowd erupted. Commentators ran out of words. But Katie barely flinched. She had lived that race a thousand times before in an empty practice pool where nobody was filming. She swam approximately 50 miles every single week. That is like swimming from one city to the next, lap after boring lap. When reporters asked her secret, she gave the most beautifully simple answer: she just never stopped showing up.

Katie, who grew up attending Catholic school and has spoken openly about her faith, understood Galatians 6:9 in her bones. Do not grow weary. The harvest is coming. She did not need the training to feel exciting. She needed it to be consistent. Every flip turn, every breath stroke, every monotonous morning was a seed planted in soil nobody could see yet.

This one is for you if training feels repetitive and dull. You are running the same drills at practice. You are shooting the same free throws. You are doing the same footwork patterns until your brain goes numb. And a voice inside whispers, "This is pointless." That voice is lying. The repetition is not the enemy of greatness. It is the builder of greatness. Katie did not become the fastest distance swimmer alive because one magical day everything clicked. She became unstoppable because she fell in love with boring consistency.

So the next time your workout feels stale, smile. You are doing exactly what champions do. You are planting invisible seeds that will bloom when the spotlight finally turns on. God does not waste a single faithful rep. He sees every quiet lap and every unglamorous drill. Your boring Tuesday practice is the beautiful foundation of your future breakthrough.

## Reflection:

Katie Ledecky showed you that embracing repetition and consistency creates extraordinary results. Greatness is built in the boring, faithful moments nobody celebrates. What repetitive part of your training do you secretly want to skip? How would committing fully to it change your results?

## Prayer:

Father, help me love the process and trust Your timing. Give me joy in repetition and patience for the harvest. Amen.

## Practice:

Pick your most boring drill this week. Do it with full focus and gratitude every single session. Watch your growth.

Your feedback is a true blessing!

If this book has encouraged you or helped you feel less alone, would you leave a quick review?

Even one sentence makes a huge difference and takes just a minute. As a small author, your feedback not only lifts my heart... it also helps other children of God find the support and hope they need.

Thank you for being part of this journey!

Scan this QR code with your phone to go to the review page and find this book.

Or

Go to your orders, find the book and click

"Write a product review"

Thank you <3

# 09

# LEBRON JAMES: HONORING THE TEMPLE

"Do you not know that your bodies are temples of the Holy Spirit, who is in you, whom you have received from God? You are not your own." - 1 Corinthians 6:19-20

LeBron James, the powerhouse basketball superstar who has dominated the NBA for over two decades, reportedly spends 1.5 million dollars every single year on his body. That number sounds wild until you watch him move at age 39 the same way he moved at 19. His secret is not a magic supplement. It is a commitment so deep it touches every hour of his day. LeBron sleeps eight to ten hours a night in a carefully controlled room. He hydrates with precise amounts of water and electrolytes. He eats clean, balanced meals built for performance, not pleasure. He soaks in ice baths, stretches with specialists, and treats recovery like a second full time job.

LeBron has spoken openly about thanking God for his abilities, and he clearly understands a powerful truth hidden inside 1 Corinthians 6:19. Your body is not yours to trash. It is a temple of the Holy Spirit. When God places athletic talent inside you, the way you treat your body becomes an act of worship or an act of waste. LeBron chose worship. Every green smoothie, every early bedtime, every skipped plate of junk food is his way of saying, "God, I will protect what You gave me."

Now here is where it gets real for you. You are staying up until midnight scrolling your phone. You are eating bags of chips before practice. You are skipping your cooldown stretches because they feel pointless. You are treating your body like a rental car instead of the sacred gift it actually is. Nobody is asking you to spend millions. But you can start making choices that honor the incredible machine God built for you.

Drink water instead of soda. Choose sleep over another episode. Eat something with actual nutrients before a game. Stretch after practice even when your teammates walk straight to the locker room. These tiny decisions might feel small today, but they stack up into something massive over time. LeBron did not become ageless by accident. He became ageless by treating every meal, every nap, and every recovery session as an investment in his calling.

Your body carries your dreams, your purpose, and the Spirit of the living God. Treat it like the sacred temple it is, and it will carry you further than you ever imagined possible.

## Reflection:

LeBron James proved that protecting your body through rest, nutrition, and recovery is an act of worship, not just performance strategy. What is one unhealthy habit you know is holding your body back? What will you replace it with starting today?

## Prayer:

God, remind me daily that my body is Your temple. Help me honor You through what I eat, how I rest, and how I train. Amen.

## Practice:

Tonight, put your phone down one hour before bed. Drink water, stretch, and sleep fully. Protect Your temple.

# 10

# TOM BRADY: BUILT THROUGH FAITHFULNESS

"Whoever can be trusted with very little can also be trusted with much." – Luke 16:10

The story everybody forgets about Tom Brady, the quarterback who won seven Super Bowl championships and reshaped the entire history of football, is the part where nobody wanted him. On NFL Draft Day in the year 2000, Tom sat in his living room watching name after name get called. Round one passed. Then round two. Then three, four, and five. His phone stayed completely silent. He was finally selected 199th overall, deep in the sixth round, by the New England Patriots. He was the seventh quarterback taken. Teams literally chose kickers and backup linemen before they chose Tom.

When he arrived at training camp, he was skinny, slow, and buried at the bottom of the depth chart. Cameras caught a young Tom walking up to team owner Robert Kraft and saying with quiet fire in his voice, "I'm the best decision this organization has ever made." Most people laughed. Nobody is laughing now.

Tom, who has spoken about his faith and the role of God in his journey, lived out Luke 16:10 with stunning precision. He did not demand the starting job. He earned it by being faithful with the smallest tasks. He studied film longer than anyone. He arrived at the facility before the sun came up and left long after dark. He mastered every tiny detail of the playbook. When his opportunity finally came due to an injury to the starter, he was so ridiculously prepared that he never gave the job back.

This is exactly where you might be standing right now. Maybe you are not the starter. Maybe the coach does not call your name first. Maybe you feel invisible compared to the kid with natural talent. Here is the truth that changes everything: God is watching how you handle the small stuff. Are you giving full effort in practice even though you are on the second team? Are you doing your homework with excellence even though nobody grades your hustle? Are you being faithful in the tiny, thankless moments?

The shortcut to greatness does not exist. Tom Brady was not born the greatest quarterback of all time. He was built, one overlooked rep at a time, by choosing faithfulness when nobody believed in him. If you stay trustworthy with the little things today, God will hand you bigger things tomorrow. Your draft position does not define your destiny. Your faithfulness does.

## Reflection:

Tom Brady showed that greatness is built through faithfulness in small, overlooked moments. Being trustworthy with little opens the door to much. Where are you cutting corners because the task feels too small? What would change if you gave that small thing your complete best?

## Prayer:

Lord, teach me to be faithful with every small task. I trust that You are building something great through my quiet obedience. Amen.

## Practice:

Pick one small responsibility you have been half doing. Commit to doing it with total excellence every day this week.

# 11

# ELIUD KIPCHOGE: THE MARATHON MONK

"Let us throw off everything that hinders and the sin that so easily entangles. And let us run with perseverance the race marked out for us." – Hebrews 12:1

On a cool morning in Vienna, Austria, in October 2019, Eliud Kipchoge did what the entire running world said was physically impossible. The Kenyan marathon legend crossed the finish line in 1 hour, 59 minutes, and 40 seconds. He became the first human being in recorded history to run a marathon in under two hours. As he broke the tape, a calm and radiant smile spread across his face. No screaming. No chest pounding. Just pure, peaceful joy. It was the smile of a man who had been running toward this moment his entire life.

What most people never see is how Eliud lives when the cameras are off. He stays in a simple training camp in Kaptagat, Kenya, where he sleeps in basic quarters, eats simple meals, and trains with a small group of runners. He makes his own bed. He cleans his own space. Despite being worth millions, he lives with a monk like simplicity that shocks reporters who visit. Eliud, a man of deep faith who often speaks about purpose and calling, embodies Hebrews 12:1 like a living sermon. He throws off every distraction. He strips away every unnecessary weight. And then he runs with breathtaking perseverance toward the race God placed before him.

His famous words echo with wisdom far beyond sports: "Only the disciplined ones in life are free." That sentence should stop you in your tracks. Eliud is saying that all those things you think give you freedom, the late nights, the distractions, the lazy shortcuts, are actually chains. True freedom comes when you have the discipline to stay locked in on your purpose for months and years without quitting.

You might be struggling right now with long term effort. The season feels endless. Your goals seem far away. The finish line is invisible. But Eliud trained for seventeen years before that historic run in Vienna. Seventeen years of waking up at the same time, running the same hills, eating the same foods, trusting the same God. He did not sustain that effort on willpower alone. He sustained it through purpose, faith, and a daily decision to keep going.

Your race is marked out for you. Throw off what slows you down. Simplify your focus. And run with perseverance, because the finish line is real even when you cannot see it yet.

## Reflection:

Eliud Kipchoge showed that long term perseverance and simple, focused living create history making results. Discipline is the true path to freedom. What distraction or unnecessary weight is slowing your race right now? What would it look like to throw it off today?

## Prayer:

Father, give me perseverance for the long race ahead. Help me release every distraction and run faithfully toward Your purpose. Amen.

## Practice:

Identify one distraction stealing your focus this week. Remove it completely and replace it with training or prayer time.

# 12

# USAIN BOLT: YEARS FOR SECONDS

"The race is not to the swift or the battle to the strong, but time and chance happen to them all." – Ecclesiastes 9:11

Berlin, Germany. August 16, 2009. The crowd inside the Olympic Stadium holds its collective breath. Usain Bolt, the towering Jamaican sprinter and devout Catholic who made the sign of the cross before every race, settles into his blocks for the 100 meter final at the World Championships. The starter's pistol fires. In what feels like a single heartbeat, Usain explodes down the track and crosses the finish line in 9.58 seconds. It is the fastest any human being has ever run. The world record. Lightning captured in flesh and bone.

Nine point five eight seconds. That is less time than it takes you to tie your shoes. Yet behind those seconds stood over fifteen years of intense, grueling, daily training. Usain started running competitively at age twelve. He trained through blistering Caribbean heat. He battled painful scoliosis in his spine that could have ended his career before it began. He spent thousands of hours perfecting his start, his drive phase, and his top end speed. He did wind sprints until his lungs burned and his legs felt like concrete. For every single second the world watched in amazement, there were roughly two full years of invisible preparation behind it.

Usain often pointed to the sky after his victories, giving visible glory to God. He understood Ecclesiastes 9:11 in a way that most people miss. The race is not simply given to the fastest. Time, preparation, and God's sovereign hand all play their part. Usain did not just show up fast. He showed up prepared, faithful, and surrendered to a plan much bigger than sprinting.

This one is for you if you want results right now. You want the trophy this season. You want the starting spot this week. You want the growth today. But real greatness is not microwaved. It is slow cooked. The results you are craving are being built right now in every practice you complete, every drill you push through, and every prayer you whisper when progress feels invisible.

Stop watching the clock and start trusting the process. Your 9.58 second moment is coming. It may arrive next month or next year or five years from now. But when it comes, every single hour of hidden training will explode into something the world will never forget. The preparation is not the delay. The preparation is the point. Trust God's timeline and keep running.

## Reflection:

Usain Bolt revealed that years of invisible, faithful training create seconds of unforgettable greatness. Quick results are an illusion. Patient preparation is the truth. Where are you rushing for instant results instead of trusting the process? What would patience look like in your training this week?

## Prayer:

God, teach me patience in my preparation. I trust Your timing over my urgency. Let every hidden hour count for Your glory. Amen.

## Practice:

Write down one long term goal. List three daily actions that build toward it. Commit to them for thirty days straight.

# 3: CONFIDENCE – SILENCING "YOU CAN'T"

# 13

# STEPH CURRY: POWER IN SMALLNESS

"For the Spirit God gave us does not make us timid, but gives us power, love and self-discipline." - 2 Timothy 1:7

June 2022. The TD Garden in Boston erupts with golden confetti. Steph Curry, the baby faced sharpshooter who revolutionized basketball forever, clutches the NBA Finals MVP trophy against his chest. Tears pour down his cheeks. His fourth championship ring is on its way. The kid that every major college rejected for being too small and too skinny is now standing on top of the basketball world, completely untouchable.

Rewind to high school. Steph was a scrawny guard with thin arms and a quiet game. Virginia Tech, where his famous father Dell Curry once starred, would only offer him a walk on spot. Not a scholarship. A walk on. Duke passed. UCLA passed. The big programs looked at his narrow frame and saw a liability. Only tiny Davidson College in North Carolina believed in him enough to offer a full scholarship. Most basketball fans had never even heard of Davidson.

But Steph carried something those scouts could never measure on a stopwatch or a scale. He carried 2 Timothy 1:7 in his bones. God did not give him a spirit of fear. God gave him power, love, and self discipline. Steph writes "I Can Do All Things" on his basketball shoes before every single game, a direct declaration of his faith. He grew up in a deeply Christian home, and that foundation became his armor against every voice that whispered he was not enough.

At Davidson, he exploded. He led that unknown school to the Elite Eight of the NCAA tournament, stunning the entire country. The NBA took notice. Golden State drafted him. And the rest is history, three point records, MVPs, and four championship rings, all wrapped in the frame of a man the experts said was too small to survive.

Here is your breakthrough. You have heard those voices too. Too short for the team. Too slow for the position. Too late to catch up. Those voices feel loud and real, but they are not from God. God's voice speaks power into your smallness and discipline into your doubt. The next time someone counts you out, lace up your shoes and remember what Steph wrote on his. You can do all things through the One who gives you strength. Your size is not your limit. Your God is your ceiling.

## Reflection:

Steph Curry proved that being overlooked does not mean being disqualified. God's spirit of power silences every voice that says you are not enough. What is one area where fear of being "not enough" is holding you back? How would playing with God's power instead of fear change things?

## Prayer:

Lord, replace every whisper of fear with Your voice of power. I am not too small for the plans You have for me. Amen.

## Practice:

Write "I can do all things" somewhere you will see daily. Read it before every practice and game this week.

# 14

# GIANNIS ANTETOKOUNMPO: INVISIBLE TO INVINCIBLE

"If God is for us, who can be against us?" – Romans 8:31

July 20, 2021. Giannis Antetokounmpo, the towering Greek basketball phenom known as "The Greek Freak," drops 50 points in Game 6 of the NBA Finals. Fifty. The Milwaukee Bucks win their first championship in fifty years, and Giannis falls to his knees on the court. His eyes look up. His lips move in silent prayer. The boy who once could not afford food has just delivered one of the greatest championship performances in NBA history.

Rewind to Athens, Greece. Giannis and his brother Thanasis shared a single pair of basketball shoes. They would take turns at practice because the family could not afford two pairs. His parents were Nigerian immigrants without legal papers, constantly afraid of deportation. Young Giannis sold watches, bags, and sunglasses on the streets just to help buy groceries. Some nights the family went to bed hungry. Basketball was not a career path. It was an escape from an impossible situation.

When the NBA drafted Giannis 15th overall in 2013, he was raw, lanky, and completely unknown. Commentators stumbled over his last name. Fans had never seen a single highlight. He arrived in Milwaukee with almost nothing, sending most of his early paychecks back to his family in Greece. The world of professional basketball felt like a different planet.

But Giannis clung to a truth that carried him through every moment of doubt. He has spoken openly about praying before games and trusting God's purpose for his life. Romans 8:31 became his anchor. If God is for us, who can be against us? Not poverty. Not invisibility. Not the scouts who overlooked him. Not the fans who could not pronounce his name. If the Creator of the universe is standing in your corner, no opponent on earth can write your final chapter.

This is your word today. Maybe you feel invisible on your team. Maybe you feel like you do not belong at the level you are playing. Maybe your background, your family situation, or your lack of resources makes you feel disqualified. Giannis felt every single one of those things, and he still became an NBA champion and MVP. Your circumstances are not your ceiling. God placed you exactly where you are for a reason. The invisible kid in the room might just be the one God is quietly preparing to become invincible.

## Reflection:

Giannis Antetokounmpo proved that poverty and invisibility cannot stop someone God is building. Your starting point does not determine your finish line. Where do you feel like you do not belong right now? What would change if you truly believed God placed you there on purpose?

## Prayer:

Father, when I feel invisible, remind me that You see everything. If You are for me, nothing against me can win. Amen.

## Practice:

Before your next game or practice, pray Romans 8:31 out loud. Walk in knowing God is already on your side.

# 15

# GABBY DOUGLAS: SILENCING THE CRITICS

"No weapon forged against you will prevail, and you will refute every tongue that accuses you." - Isaiah 54:17

August 2, 2012. Gabby Douglas, a sixteen year old gymnast from Virginia Beach with a radiant smile and explosive power, sticks her final landing at the London Olympics. The scoreboard flashes. She has just won the individual all around gold medal, becoming the first African American gymnast in history to claim that title. The arena roars. Her teammates rush to hug her. It is supposed to be the greatest moment of her young life.

But when Gabby turned on her phone, the world she found waiting was cruel. Instead of celebrating her historic achievement, thousands of comments online attacked her hair. Her appearance. Her skin. People who had never done a single cartwheel in their lives tore apart a girl who had just outperformed every gymnast on the planet. The criticism hit like a punch to the chest. And the worst part was not what strangers said out loud. It was what those words did inside Gabby's mind. Their voices slowly became her voice. She started doubting her own beauty, her own worth, her own belonging.

Gabby, a passionate and vocal Christian, had to fight a war that no medal could settle. She leaned deeply into her faith and clung to Isaiah 54:17. No weapon formed against her would prosper. Not the hateful tweets. Not the cruel jokes. Not even the inner voice that replayed their words on an endless loop. She spoke openly about how God's love became louder than the criticism. She realized that the enemy will always try to use outside voices to plant inside lies.

This is critical for you. Criticism is coming. It might already be here. A coach who says something harsh. A teammate who makes a cutting joke. A comment section full of strangers with opinions about your body, your skills, or your worth. The real danger is not what they say out loud. The real danger is when you start repeating it to yourself in the quiet of your own mind.

Here is the truth. If God says no weapon formed against you will succeed, then every cruel word has an expiration date. Let it expire. Do not adopt the voices of people who have never walked in your shoes. Guard your inner voice like a fortress. Speak God's truth over yourself until it drowns out every lie. Gabby won Olympic gold and then won something even harder. She won the battle for her own mind.

## Reflection:

Gabby Douglas taught you that outside criticism becomes truly dangerous only when it becomes your inner voice. God's truth must be louder than any lie. Whose negative words have you been replaying in your mind? What specific truth from God can you use to replace that voice today?

## Prayer:

Lord, silence the lies I have been believing. Let Your truth be the loudest voice in my mind and heart. Amen.

## Practice:

Write one negative thought you keep replaying. Cross it out. Replace it with one Scripture truth. Read it every morning.

# 16
# ALLYSON FELIX: AN UNPLANNED STORY

"God is within her, she will not fall; God will help her at break of day." – Psalm 46:5

Allyson Felix stood on the Olympic podium in Tokyo in 2021, a bronze medal hanging around her neck for the 400 meters, and every step that brought her there had been soaked in tears most people never saw. The most decorated American track and field athlete in history, with eleven Olympic medals to her name, was not supposed to be standing there at all. Two years earlier, her body had written a story she never planned.

In November 2018, Allyson was thirty two weeks pregnant when her blood pressure spiked to dangerous levels. Doctors diagnosed severe preeclampsia. Her daughter Camryn had to be delivered by emergency C section at just three pounds. Tiny, fragile, and fighting for life. Allyson lay in that hospital bed, her abdomen cut open, her baby in the intensive care unit, and her entire identity as an athlete suddenly uncertain. The legs that had carried her to nine Olympic medals could barely carry her down the hospital hallway.

Allyson, a deeply devoted Christian who has spoken boldly about her relationship with Jesus, held onto Psalm 46:5 like a lifeline. God is within her. She will not fall. That promise did not mean the pain would disappear. It meant she would not be destroyed by it. Recovery was brutal. Her core had been surgically split open. Running felt foreign in her own body. She had to relearn movement patterns she had mastered since childhood.

But Allyson did not just come back to the track. She came back with a fiercer purpose. She fought Nike publicly for fair maternity protections for female athletes. She launched her own shoe brand. She became a voice for mothers everywhere. And then she went to Tokyo and won two more medals, becoming the most decorated U.S. track athlete in Olympic history.

Maybe your body has thrown you a curveball you did not expect. An injury. A growth spurt that changed your coordination. A medical condition that altered your training. Maybe puberty is reshaping everything and your sport suddenly feels different. You did not plan this chapter. But God is still writing your story. Your body changing does not mean your purpose is canceled. It means your purpose is being refined. Allyson proved that the hardest chapter can become the most powerful one. God is within you. You will not fall.

## Reflection:

Allyson Felix showed that when your body writes a story you did not plan, God's presence keeps you standing. Hardship refines your purpose. What unexpected change in your body or health has shaken your confidence? How can trusting God through it change your perspective today?

## Prayer:

God, when my body feels uncertain, anchor my identity in You. You are within me and I will not fall. Amen.

## Practice:

Name one physical challenge you are facing. Pray Psalm 46:5 over it tonight. Then take one recovery step tomorrow.

# 17

# BROCK PURDY: CHOSEN NOT IRRELEVANT

"My grace is sufficient for you, for my power is made perfect in weakness." - 2 Corinthians 12:9-10

April 30, 2022. The NFL Draft has been running for three long days. Two hundred and sixty one names have already been called. Television cameras swing to a young quarterback from Iowa State sitting with his family, waiting through an agonizing silence. Then the announcement comes. With the 262nd and final pick, the San Francisco 49ers select Brock Purdy. He is officially "Mr. Irrelevant," the title given to the very last player chosen in the entire draft. The least wanted. The afterthought. The name nobody expects to remember.

Less than eight months later, Brock Purdy stood in a huddle at Levi's Stadium calling plays for one of the most explosive offenses in football. Every quarterback ahead of him on the depth chart had gone down with injuries, and Brock, the last pick, stepped in and started winning. And winning. And winning. He led the 49ers to the NFC Championship in his rookie season and then all the way to the Super Bowl the following year. Mr. Irrelevant became Mr. Undeniable.

Brock is a deeply committed Christian who has been vocal about his faith since his college days at Iowa State. He has talked openly about how 2 Corinthians 12:9 shaped his identity long before the NFL ever called his name. God's power is made perfect in weakness. Brock did not need to be the first pick to fulfill his purpose. In fact, being the last pick became the very platform God used to display His power. When the world labels you irrelevant, God whispers, "Perfect. Now watch what I do."

This hits hard if you have ever been the last one picked. Last to make the roster. Last to get called off the bench. Last in the rankings. That label stings. It can crawl inside your chest and convince you that you do not matter. But Brock Purdy carried that label into an NFL stadium and turned it into a testimony. He did not run from the title. He redeemed it.

Your weakness is not a disqualification. It is an invitation for God's power to show up in a way nobody can deny. Stop begging for the world's approval and start trusting God's assignment. The last pick is still picked. You are still chosen. And sometimes being counted out is the greatest setup for a God sized comeback that leaves everyone speechless.

## Reflection:

Brock Purdy proved that being last picked does not mean being least valued. God's power shows up strongest when the world counts you out. Where has imposter syndrome made you feel like you do not belong? What changes if you believe God chose you for this exact moment?

## Prayer:

Lord, when I feel like the last choice, remind me that Your power shines brightest through my weakness. I am chosen. Amen.

## Practice:

Write "Chosen, not irrelevant" on a card. Place it in your locker or bag. Read it before every competition this week.

# 18

# TYSON FURY: FROM PIT TO KING

"I waited patiently for the Lord; he turned to me and heard my cry. He lifted me out of the slimy pit, out of the mud and mire; he set my feet on a rock and gave me a firm place to stand." - Psalm 40:1-2

In June 2018, Tyson Fury, the massive six foot nine British heavyweight boxer who had once stunned the world by defeating the legendary Wladimir Klitschko for the world title, was sitting alone in a dark room, weighing nearly 400 pounds. He had not trained in over two years. He was drinking heavily. Depression had wrapped itself around his mind like a thick, suffocating fog. He later admitted publicly that he drove his Ferrari at high speed toward a bridge, ready to end everything. At the very last second, he heard a voice telling him to stop. He believes with all his heart that voice was God.

That moment became the turning point of his entire life. Tyson, who calls himself "The Gypsy King" and speaks about Jesus Christ with raw, unfiltered passion, began the slow and painful climb out of the darkest pit imaginable. He started training again, one painful session at a time. He lost over 130 pounds. He opened up publicly about his mental health struggles, something almost unheard of in the tough world of heavyweight boxing. And he clung to Psalm 40 like a drowning man gripping a rescue rope. God heard his cry. God reached into the mud and pulled him out. God set his feet on solid rock.

In February 2020, Tyson Fury stood in the ring in Las Vegas and knocked out Deontay Wilder to reclaim the heavyweight championship of the world. He sang "American Pie" to the crowd. He wept. He praised God in every interview. The man who almost ended his life was now standing on top of it.

If dark thoughts haunt you, please hear this clearly. You are not broken. You are not alone. And you are not too far gone for God to reach. Depression, anxiety, and heavy sadness are real battles, and pretending they do not exist does not make them disappear. But there is a God who specializes in pulling people out of pits. He does not wait for you to clean yourself up first. He meets you in the mud.

Talk to someone you trust. A parent, a coach, a counselor, a pastor. Let them in. Your bravest moment might not be a game winning play. It might be the moment you finally say, "I need help." That is the knockout punch that changes everything.

## Reflection:

Tyson Fury showed that even the deepest darkness cannot separate you from God's rescue. Asking for help is the bravest fight you will ever win. If dark thoughts or heavy feelings are weighing you down, who is one safe person you can talk to honestly this week?

## Prayer:

Father, lift me from every dark pit. Set my feet on Your rock. Remind me I am never too broken for Your love. Amen.

## Practice:

If you are struggling, tell one trusted person this week. If you are well, check on one friend who might not be okay.

# 4: PRESSURE — WHEN IT MATTERS MOST

# 19

# CLAYTON KERSHAW: TRUSTING THE PATH

"Trust in the Lord with all your heart and lean not on your own understanding; in all your ways submit to him, and he will make your paths straight." - Proverbs 3:5-6

Clayton Kershaw stands on the pitcher's mound at Globe Life Field in Arlington, Texas, gripping a fresh baseball in his left hand. The Los Angeles Dodgers just won the 2020 World Series, and tears stream down his face. Confetti drifts through the cool October air like golden snow. His teammates pile onto each other in wild celebration. But Clayton's mind flashes back to every painful October before this moment. The blown leads. The bold headlines. The single word that haunted him for years: choker.

Clayton Kershaw, one of the greatest pitchers in baseball history, dominated the regular season year after year. Three Cy Young Awards. An MVP trophy. Unhittable stuff that left batters shaking their heads. But when October arrived, something seemed to shift. He gave up crushing home runs in the biggest moments. Sportswriters built an entire storyline around his failures. Fans questioned his heart. The label "postseason choker" followed him everywhere like a shadow he could not shake.

But Clayton never stopped trusting God's path for his life. He and his wife Ellen built orphanages and served communities across the globe through their faith. He held tightly to Proverbs 3:5-6 like a promise carved in stone: if you trust God completely and stop leaning on your own limited understanding, He will make your path straight. Clayton stopped trying to control every outcome on the mound. He surrendered the results to God and focused only on preparation and faithfulness to the process.

This is exactly what you need to hear. Maybe you missed the free throw that lost the game. Maybe you struck out with the bases loaded and heard the crowd go painfully silent. You replay it every night. You tell yourself you are destined to fail when it matters most. That is a lie. One bad moment does not write your whole story. Clayton had a full decade of painful Octobers, and God still made his path straight. Your job is not to guarantee the result. Your job is to prepare, trust, and release the pressure to the One who holds every outcome in His hands. Choking is not your identity. It is just one chapter. Keep pitching.

## Reflection:

Clayton Kershaw proved that past failures do not define your future. Trusting God's plan freed him from the crushing weight of a painful label. When you replay a failure, are you leaning on your own feelings or trusting God's bigger plan for your story?

## Prayer:

Lord, take my fear of failure. I trust Your path, not my painful past. Straighten my steps today. Amen.

## Practice:

Write down one past failure. Beside it write: "This does not define me. God is still directing my path."

# 20

# COCO GAUFF: CASTING EVERY ANXIETY

"Cast all your anxiety on him because he cares for you." – 1 Peter 5:7

Coco Gauff, fifteen years old, stands on the sacred grass of Wimbledon's Centre Court. She has just defeated Venus Williams, one of the greatest tennis players who ever lived. The crowd erupts with shocked, joyful cheering. Coco's wide brown eyes shimmer with disbelief. She presses both hands over her mouth as tears spill down her sunlit cheeks. The entire sports world is watching this moment. A teenager just beat a living legend. And now everyone expects her to keep winning.

The overnight fame was electric. But the weight that followed was crushing. Coco Gauff, the young tennis phenom from Delray Beach, Florida, suddenly had millions of eyes tracking every forehand, every facial expression, every single loss. Reporters compared her to Serena Williams. Social media exploded after matches. Sponsors lined up at the door. And behind all that glittering attention, a fifteen-year-old girl was just trying to breathe.

Coco grew up in a strong Christian household and has always been vocal about her faith. She writes Bible verses on her shoes before matches. After tough losses she turns to worship music instead of scrolling through painful comments online. She clings to 1 Peter

5:7 like a steady anchor: cast all your anxiety on Him because He cares for you. Coco learned early that carrying the world's expectations by herself would crush her spirit completely. So she hands that weight to God. Every single time.

Here is the truth for you. Maybe your coach just promoted you to varsity. Maybe you won a big tournament and suddenly everyone expects you to win every time. Maybe your parents, your teammates, or your classmates put pressure on you that makes your chest tight and your stomach twist into knots. You feel like you cannot afford one bad game because everyone is watching now. That weight was never yours to carry. God did not design your shoulders to hold the world's opinions. He designed them to be lifted toward Him in surrender. Coco still loses matches. She still cries after hard nights. But she never carries the anxiety alone. The next time pressure squeezes your ribs before a big moment, picture yourself physically handing that heavy weight to God. He is already reaching for it. Let go.

## Reflection:

Coco Gauff teaches that expectations from others do not belong on your shoulders. God invites you to release that crushing pressure to Him completely. What expectation are you carrying right now that you need to hand over to God before your next competition?

## Prayer:

Father, I cast every anxious thought on You. You care for me deeply. Carry what I cannot carry alone. Amen.

## Practice:

Before your next game, write "1 Peter 5:7" on your wrist or shoe. Let it remind you to release pressure to God.

# 21

# MICHAEL JORDAN: THE BRAVE SHOT

"Have I not commanded you? Be strong and courageous. Do not be afraid; do not be discouraged, for the Lord your God will be with you wherever you go." - Joshua 1:9

Michael Jordan. The name alone makes basketball fans hold their breath. Six NBA championships. Five MVP awards. Some of the most clutch moments in sports history. But here is the scene most people forget. A skinny sophomore in Wilmington, North Carolina, walks up to a list pinned on a gymnasium wall. His eyes scan desperately for his name. It is not there. Michael Jordan was cut from his varsity basketball team. He walked home, shut his bedroom door, and cried until his pillow was soaked.

That rejection could have buried him. Instead, it ignited something fierce inside his heart. Michael Jordan became the greatest basketball player to ever touch a court, and he built his legendary career on one burning belief: he would never run from the biggest moments. He took the last shot when his hands were shaking. He demanded the ball when the scoreboard was tight and the clock was bleeding final seconds. He missed over 9,000 shots across his career. He lost nearly 300 games. He missed 26 game-winning shots that could have been highlight reels. And none of that stopped him from wanting the ball again.

Jordan has spoken about believing that God blessed him with a gift and a purpose greater than basketball. Joshua 1:9 echoes perfectly through his competitive spirit: be strong, be courageous, do not be afraid. God did not promise that every shot would fall cleanly through the net. He promised that He would be with you wherever you go. The courage is not found in the result. The courage lives in the willingness to step forward when everyone else steps back.

Maybe you freeze when the pressure hits. The penalty kick. The final inning. The last possession. Your legs feel like wet cement. Your thoughts race in wild circles. You secretly wish someone else would take the responsibility. But God did not place you in that moment by accident. He positioned you there on purpose. The last shot mentality is not about being perfect. It is about being willing. It is about declaring, "I might miss, but I refuse to hide." Every time you step into a pressure moment with courage, you are training your faith muscles. You are proving that God's presence matters more than any scoreboard. Take the shot. He is already with you.

## Reflection:

Michael Jordan showed that courage is not the absence of fear but the willingness to act anyway. God commands strength because He guarantees His presence. When was the last time you hid from a big moment, and what would change if you trusted God was standing right beside you?

## Prayer:

God, make me brave in the biggest moments. I will not hide. You are with me wherever I go. Amen.

## Practice:

This week, volunteer to take the big shot, the tough play, or the hard assignment. Step forward and trust God's presence.

# 22
# PATRICK MAHOMES: THE COMEBACK KING

"So do not fear, for I am with you; do not be dismayed, for I am your God. I will strengthen you and help you; I will uphold you with my righteous right hand." - Isaiah 41:10

Super Bowl LIV. Fourth quarter. The San Francisco 49ers lead 20 to 10, and their defense looks absolutely unbreakable. Millions of viewers start clicking off their televisions. The game feels finished. But on the Kansas City Chiefs sideline, a 24-year-old quarterback with wild curly hair and fearless eyes gathers his teammates into a tight huddle. Patrick Mahomes looks each one of them directly in the face and says something simple: we are going to win this game.

What happened next still sends chills down spines years later. Mahomes launched three consecutive touchdown drives in the final seven minutes to win 31 to 20 and capture his first Super Bowl championship. He screamed into the cameras with pure fire. Golden confetti rained down on him. He was named Super Bowl MVP. But this was not some lucky hot streak. Patrick Mahomes, the star quarterback of the Kansas City Chiefs, built his entire career around one unshakable belief: no deficit is final.

Patrick has spoken about his faith openly, crediting God for his talent and his path. Isaiah 41:10 lives inside his competitive spirit like fuel in an engine. Do not fear. God is with you. He will strengthen you. He will hold you up. Mahomes does not panic when the scoreboard turns ugly. He does not pout on the sideline or point fingers when things fall apart. He trusts completely that the game is not over until it is truly over.

You need this fire burning in your life. Maybe your team is down by three goals at halftime. Maybe your grades are slipping and it feels too late to recover. Maybe you lost the first set and your legs feel like heavy concrete. That sinking feeling whispers, "Just give up. It is already done." That whisper is a flat-out lie. God does not abandon you when the scoreboard looks ugly. He stands right beside you with fresh strength for the very next play. A comeback is not about talent alone. It is about refusing to quit because you know who holds you up with His mighty hand. Do not shut down. Take a deep breath, lock your eyes on the next play, and let God fuel the comeback. The game is never over with Him on your side.

## Reflection:

Patrick Mahomes proved that deficits do not determine destiny. God promises to strengthen you and hold you up no matter how far behind you feel. When you fall behind, do you shut down or look for the next play? What would trusting God in that moment actually look like?

## Prayer:

Lord, when I fall behind, remind me You are still here. Strengthen me for the next play. I will not quit. Amen.

## Practice:

Next time you are losing, say out loud: "This is not over." Then focus only on the very next play in front of you.

# 23.
# COOPER KUPP: PRAYER EVERY SNAP

"Do not be anxious about anything, but in every situation, by prayer and petition, with thanksgiving, present your requests to God. And the peace of God, which transcends all understanding, will guard your hearts and your minds in Christ Jesus." - Philippians 4:6-7

Super Bowl LVI. The Los Angeles Rams trail the Cincinnati Bengals with under two minutes remaining. The ball spirals through the thick stadium air and finds Cooper Kupp's reliable hands in the back of the end zone. The stadium shakes with a deafening roar. He clutches the football against his chest, drops to one knee, and points straight up toward heaven. That touchdown sealed the championship. Cooper Kupp, the wide receiver from Yakima, Washington, was named Super Bowl MVP. But that shining trophy was not the most important thing he carried off the field that night.

Cooper Kupp is one of the most openly faithful athletes in professional football. Before every single snap, he prays. Not long, dramatic prayers performed for the cameras. Quick, honest conversations with God. "Give me peace. Help me focus. Thank You for this moment." It is a rhythm as natural as breathing. Cooper has shared that without that constant connection to God during the game, anxiety would swallow him completely. The speed of the NFL is blinding. Defenders are faster than anything you can imagine. The noise of 70,000 screaming fans can turn your sharpest thoughts into total static. Cooper's secret weapon against all of it is simple, steady prayer.

Philippians 4:6-7 is his heartbeat on the field. Do not be anxious about anything. Pray about everything. And God's peace, a peace that does not even make logical sense, will guard your heart and your mind. Cooper does not wait until the final whistle to talk to God. He talks to God during every single play of the game.

Here is your challenge. You probably forget about God the second the whistle blows. Your mind locks onto the score, the opponent, the crowd, the mistakes piling up. God becomes a pregame thought or a postgame thank-you. But He wants to be with you between the lines. He wants to hear from you at halftime when your confidence is trembling. He wants you whispering to Him before the free throw, between sets, during the timeout. Prayer is not a religious ritual you perform. It is a living lifeline. Start talking to God during the game, not just before and after it. You will feel a peace that no scoreboard can explain. He is listening right now.

## Reflection:

Cooper Kupp shows that prayer belongs inside the game, not just before and after. God wants to be your constant companion during every intense competitive moment. Do you only talk to God before and after games, or are you inviting Him into the pressure of every single play?

## Prayer:

God, remind me to talk to You during the game. Fill me with peace that passes all understanding right now. Amen.

## Practice:

During your next practice, whisper a short prayer before one key play. Notice the peace it brings. Build the habit.

# 24

# JALEN HURTS: BENCHED BUT UNSTOPPABLE

"When I am afraid, I put my trust in you." - Psalm 56:3

The SEC Championship Game, 2018. Alabama trails Georgia and the crowd noise is deafening. The starting quarterback is injured. Suddenly Jalen Hurts jogs onto the field. The same Jalen Hurts who was benched months earlier in the National Championship. The same Jalen Hurts who watched silently from the sideline as Tua Tagovailoa took his starting job. The same Jalen Hurts who stayed when everyone expected him to leave and never look back. He leads Alabama to a stunning comeback victory, and when the final whistle screams, his teammates swarm him with fierce love. Tears fill his eyes. Not tears of bitterness. Tears of faithfulness rewarded.

Jalen Hurts, the quarterback from Channelview, Texas, knows exactly what it feels like to have everything stripped away. He was the starting quarterback at the University of Alabama who led his team to back-to-back National Championship appearances. Then, in the biggest game of his life, his coach pulled him at halftime and replaced him with a true freshman. The cameras caught Jalen's face on the sideline. It looked absolutely crushed. But what Jalen did next shocked the entire sports world. He stayed. He supported Tua publicly. He showed up to practice every single day, lifted heavy weights, studied film for hours, and cheered louder than anyone on the bench.

Jalen has always been vocal about his deep faith. Psalm 56:3 is his bedrock foundation. When I am afraid, I put my trust in You. He did not trust his own stinging emotions after being benched. He did not let fear or growing bitterness make his decisions. He handed his raw pain directly to God and kept working in faithful silence.

After that heroic SEC Championship rescue, Jalen transferred to Oklahoma, finished as a Heisman Trophy finalist, and eventually became the franchise quarterback of the Philadelphia Eagles, leading them all the way to the Super Bowl.

If you have ever been benched, overlooked, or replaced, listen carefully. Your setback is not your sentence. The bench is not a burial ground. It is a training ground. God is not done writing your story just because someone else got your spot. Stay faithful exactly where you are. Keep grinding when nobody is watching. Trust God with your fear and your frustration. Jalen did not run from the painful season. He walked straight through it with God, and God opened doors no human being could ever shut.

## Reflection:

Jalen Hurts showed that being benched is not the end. Trusting God through rejection and staying faithful positioned him for something far greater ahead. If you are on the bench right now, are you letting bitterness take root or trusting God to use this season for explosive growth?

## Prayer:

Lord, when I am afraid and overlooked, I choose to trust You. My setback is not my ending. Use me. Amen.

## Practice:

If you are not starting, encourage a teammate today. Stay faithful in the small role. Trust God with the bigger picture.

# 5: RESILIENCE — RISE AGAIN

# 25

# DAMAR HAMLIN: MIRACLE ON TURF

"I will not die but live, and will proclaim what the Lord has done."
- Psalm 118:17

Seventy million people watched. The lights of Paycor Stadium in Cincinnati blazed across the field on that freezing January Monday night. Damar Hamlin, the 24-year-old Buffalo Bills safety, was playing NFL football on the biggest stage of his young career. He sprinted toward the ball carrier, wrapped him up in a textbook tackle, and popped back to his feet. Then something no one expected happened. Damar took two steps and collapsed face-first onto the frozen turf. His heart had stopped.

Medical teams sprinted across the field. Players from both the Bills and the Bengals dropped to their knees in prayer right there on the grass. Grown men sobbed openly. The stadium fell completely silent except for the desperate sound of paramedics performing CPR on Damar's chest. An ambulance rolled onto the field. Millions of viewers at home pressed their hands together and begged God for a miracle.

God answered.

Days later, Damar woke up in the hospital. Tubes covered his body. Machines beeped beside him. But his eyes were open, and his first scribbled question on a notepad made the nurses laugh through their tears: "Did we win?" When he could finally speak, Damar pointed one finger toward heaven and told the world that

God had given him a second chance. He clung to Psalm 118:17 like a lifeline, declaring that he would not die but live and proclaim what the Lord had done.

The hardest part was not surviving. It was stepping back onto the field. Fear told Damar to stay home, stay safe, never risk another hit. But the following NFL season, Damar suited up and played again. He felt the fear and chose faith over it.

Maybe something terrifying has happened to you. A violent collision. A scary medical moment. A panic attack before a big game. That fear wants to lock you in a cage and throw away the key. But your story is not over. God did not bring you through the fire just to leave you sitting in the ashes. He brought you through so you could stand back up and declare His goodness.

Feel the fear. Acknowledge it honestly. Then lace up your shoes and walk straight through it, because the God who restarted Damar Hamlin's heart is the same God walking beside you right now.

## Reflection:

Damar Hamlin showed you that surviving something terrifying is not the finish line. Trusting God enough to return to the field is where real courage lives. What fear from a past experience is keeping you on the sideline, and what would stepping back onto the field look like for you?

## Prayer:

Lord, You gave me life for a purpose. When fear freezes me, thaw my heart with Your courage. I trust You. Amen.

## Practice:

Write Psalm 118:17 somewhere visible. This week, take one brave step toward the thing that scares you most.

# 26

# ALEX SMITH: FORGED IN FIRE

"We also glory in our sufferings, because we know that suffering produces perseverance; perseverance, character; and character, hope." - Romans 5:3-5

The roar inside FedEx Field shook the ground beneath Alex Smith's cleats. The Washington Football Team quarterback dropped back, scanned the field, and completed a clean spiral downfield. The crowd leaped to its feet. Not because of the throw itself, but because of who was throwing it. Two years earlier, doctors told Alex he might never walk normally again. Now he was playing NFL football. That single pass was a miracle disguised as a spiral.

On November 18, 2018, Alex suffered one of the most gruesome injuries in football history. During a game against the Houston Texans, his right leg snapped in a compound fracture. The bone pierced through his skin. But that was only the beginning of his nightmare. A flesh-eating bacterial infection invaded the wound. Doctors performed surgery after surgery after surgery. Seventeen surgeries total. They rebuilt his leg using muscle from other parts of his body. At one dark point, they told him amputation was a real possibility. Alex nearly lost his leg. He nearly lost his life.

Through every single procedure, Alex held tightly to Romans 5:3-5. Suffering was producing something powerful inside him. Each painful surgery built perseverance. Each grueling rehab session forged character. And character kept filling his chest with a hope that refused to die. Alex told reporters that his faith in God was the anchor keeping him steady when everything else was falling apart.

Most people would have accepted a comfortable retirement. Nobody would have blamed him. But Alex spent seventeen months relearning how to walk, then how to run, then how to throw. He returned to the NFL in 2020 and led Washington to the playoffs. He was named Comeback Player of the Year.

Maybe right now your injury feels like the final chapter. The crutches. The long rehab timeline. The games you are missing. It feels like your dream is slipping away with every day spent on the sideline. But God does not waste your suffering. He is using every painful moment to build something unbreakable inside you. Perseverance. Character. Hope.

Your injury is not the end of your story. It is the chapter where the hero gets forged in fire. Trust the pain. Trust the process. Trust the God who turns seventeen surgeries into an incredible miracle.

## Reflection:

Alex Smith proved that even the most devastating injury cannot destroy a dream God is protecting. Suffering builds endurance, character, and unstoppable hope. What setback or injury are you facing right now, and how might God be using it to build something stronger inside you?

## Prayer:

Father, when my body breaks and hope fades, remind me You are building something unbreakable inside me. I trust Your plan. Amen.

## Practice:

Write one thing your current struggle is teaching you. Read Romans 5:3-5 every morning this week and watch your perspective shift.

# 27

# JOSH HAMILTON: NEW MORNING MERCY

"Because of the Lord's great love we are not consumed, for his compassions never fail. They are new every morning; great is your faithfulness." - Lamentations 3:22-23

The crack of the bat echoed through Rangers Ballpark like a thunderclap. Josh Hamilton, the Texas Rangers outfielder, sent a baseball soaring deep into the July night sky during the 2008 Home Run Derby. Ball after ball rocketed off his bat. The crowd counted each blast louder and louder. He crushed 28 home runs in the first round alone. It was the most spectacular display of raw power anyone had ever witnessed. But the real miracle was not the home runs. The real miracle was that Josh Hamilton was alive at all.

Nine years earlier, Josh was the number one overall pick in the 1999 MLB Draft. He was supposed to be baseball's next superstar. But instead of reaching the big leagues, Josh fell into a pit of drug and alcohol addiction that swallowed him whole. He lost everything. His career. His money. His family. His dignity. He slept in strangers' houses and woke up on cold floors with no memory of the night before. He was banned from baseball entirely. For years, nobody believed Josh Hamilton would ever play a single professional game.

At his absolute lowest, broken and completely hollow, Josh cried out to God. And God reached down into that pit. Josh described his salvation as the moment everything changed. He surrendered his life to Jesus and entered recovery. The road back was brutal and humbling. Every single morning, Josh had to choose faith over his cravings. He clung to Lamentations 3:22-23, believing God's compassions were waiting for him with each new sunrise. New morning. New mercy. Complete fresh start.

Josh returned to professional baseball and became the 2010 American League MVP. His testimony shook the sports world because it proved that no pit is too deep for God's hand to reach.

Maybe you feel like you have hit rock bottom. Maybe it is not addiction but failure, depression, or total exhaustion. Maybe you feel too far gone for anyone to believe in you, including yourself. But the same God who pulled Josh Hamilton out of darkness is offering you new mercy right now, this morning.

You are not defined by your worst chapter. Rock bottom is not your permanent address. It is the foundation God uses to rebuild something beautiful. Open your eyes tomorrow and say out loud, "His compassions are new this morning." Then get up and take one step forward.

## Reflection:

Josh Hamilton showed you that no pit is too deep for God to reach. Every new morning carries fresh mercy and a genuine chance to start again. Where do you feel stuck at rock bottom, and are you willing to let God's mercy meet you fresh tomorrow morning?

## Prayer:

God, Your mercy is new every single morning. When I feel too far gone, pull me up and grant me a fresh start. Amen.

## Practice:

Tomorrow morning, before anything else, say aloud: "His compassions are new today." Repeat every morning this week and notice the shift.

# 28

# CARSON WENTZ: BENCHED NOT BROKEN

"Wait for the Lord; be strong and take heart and wait for the Lord." – Psalm 27:14

The confetti fell in slow motion. Green and white streamers danced through the cold February air inside U.S. Bank Stadium in Minneapolis. The Philadelphia Eagles had just won Super Bowl LII. The entire city would celebrate for weeks. But one player watched from the sideline wearing street clothes, his knee wrapped in a heavy brace. Carson Wentz, the Eagles' franchise quarterback, stood close enough to touch the Lombardi Trophy but felt a million miles away from the victory.

Weeks earlier, Carson had been playing the best football of his life. He was the frontrunner for the NFL's Most Valuable Player award. His arm was electric. His confidence soared. Then, in a December game against the Los Angeles Rams, he tore his ACL. Just like that, his magical season was over. His backup, Nick Foles, stepped in and led the Eagles to a championship while Carson watched helplessly from the bench.

The years that followed were even harder. Carson was traded to Indianapolis, then to Washington. He lost starting jobs. Critics questioned his talent. Fans who once chanted his name debated whether he belonged in the league. For a young man who built his entire identity around being "the guy," losing that role felt like losing himself.

But Carson did not crumble. Throughout every setback, he anchored himself to Psalm 27:14 and to his foundation called AO1, which stands for Audience of One. Carson reminded himself constantly that he played for God's approval alone, not the crowd's applause. Waiting on the Lord did not mean sitting still and doing nothing. It meant working hard while trusting God's timing instead of demanding his own.

Maybe you have lost your starting spot. Maybe someone else got the position, the role, the recognition that you earned through sweat and sacrifice. It stings deeply. It makes you question your worth and wonder if all your effort was pointless. But hear this clearly: your value was never determined by your spot on the roster. God sees you working when nobody else is watching.

Being benched does not mean being forgotten. It means being prepared. Keep your heart strong. Keep your hands ready. Your moment is not canceled. It is simply loading. Wait on the Lord, and He will renew your strength.

## Reflection:

Carson Wentz taught you that losing your starting spot does not erase your value. Playing for an audience of one means your worth comes from God, not your position. When have you tied your identity to a role, and how would your confidence change if you truly played for God's approval alone?

## Prayer:

Lord, when I lose my place, anchor my worth in You alone. Teach me to wait with strength and keep my heart ready. Amen.

## Practice:

Write "Audience of One" on your wrist or notebook. Before every practice this week, remind yourself that God's approval is the only ranking that matters.

# 29

# TUA TAGOVAILOA: PLAYING THROUGH FEAR

"Be strong and courageous. Do not be afraid or terrified because of them, for the Lord your God goes with you; he will never leave you nor forsake you." - Deuteronomy 31:6

The stadium lights at Hard Rock Stadium reflected off Tua Tagovailoa's helmet as the young quarterback jogged back onto the field. His legs looked steady, but his mind was fighting a battle nobody could see. Just months earlier, the Miami Dolphins quarterback had been carried off a football field on a stretcher after a terrifying concussion left his fingers locked in an unnatural position while 65,000 fans watched in horrified silence. The image replayed on every sports channel for days. Doctors warned him. Commentators debated his future. Everyone had an opinion about whether Tua should ever play again.

But Tua kept stepping onto the field.

Growing up in a Samoan Christian household in Hawaii, Tua's faith was woven into his identity long before he ever picked up a football. His family prayed together constantly. When Tua arrived at the University of Alabama, he entered the 2018 National Championship game as a true freshman and threw a walk-off overtime touchdown to win it all. That moment launched his career into orbit. But the injuries that followed tested everything he believed.

A devastating hip injury during his junior season at Alabama nearly ended his football future before the NFL even started. Then came the concussions in Miami. Each hit brought new questions. Each recovery brought new fear. The whispers grew louder everywhere: "Walk away. Protect yourself. It is not worth it."

Tua responded by leaning deeper into Deuteronomy 31:6. God had not promised him a life free from danger. God promised something greater: His presence directly in the middle of it. Be strong. Be courageous. I am with you. That promise did not remove the risk, but it completely redefined how Tua walked through it. He competed not because the fear disappeared but because his faith was bigger than his fear.

You might know this feeling. The memory of a bad hit, a twisted ankle, or a painful fall replaying in your mind every time you step on the field. Your body has healed but your brain keeps flinching. Courage is not the absence of fear. Courage is trusting that God walks beside you directly into the moments that terrify you most.

He will never leave you. He will never forsake you. Play through the fear, because He is already on the field waiting for you.

## Reflection:

Tua Tagovailoa showed you that courage is not competing without fear. It is competing with fear and trusting God is right beside you through every hit. What physical or emotional fear keeps replaying in your mind, and how would trusting God's presence change the way you compete?

## Prayer:

God, You promised to never leave me. When fear screams, speak louder. Give me courage to play boldly through it. Amen.

## Practice:

Before your next game, close your eyes and whisper Deuteronomy 31:6. Picture God beside you on the field. Then go compete fearlessly.

# 30

# AARON JUDGE: RISING FROM SLUMPS

"For though the righteous fall seven times, they rise again." - Proverbs 24:16

The crack was unmistakable. Aaron Judge, the towering New York Yankees outfielder, watched the baseball disappear over the left field wall at Globe Life Field in Arlington, Texas. Home run number 62. The American League record. The stadium erupted. His teammates mobbed him at home plate. Cameras flashed from every direction. Aaron pumped his fist and embraced his mother in the stands, tears streaming down her face. It was one of the most electric moments in baseball history.

But rewind the tape a few weeks, and the picture looks completely different.

Before that record-breaking blast, Aaron endured one of the most public and painful slumps of his career. After hitting home run number 60, the entire world stopped to watch every single at-bat. Every pitch. Every swing. Networks showed split-screen coverage of his every movement. And Aaron went cold. For nearly two agonizing weeks he could not connect. He struck out. He grounded out. He popped up weakly. Reporters asked the same question after every game: "When will you break the record?" The pressure was absolutely suffocating.

Through it all, Aaron stayed patient. The 6-foot-7 slugger spoke openly about his Christian faith and his belief that God's timing was perfect even when his bat was not. He reminded himself of Proverbs 24:16: a righteous person falls seven times but rises again. Aaron understood that falling was not the failure. Staying down was the failure. So he kept stepping into the batter's box. He kept swinging. He kept trusting.

When you are stuck in a slump, everything feels impossibly heavy. Your confidence shrinks with every missed shot, failed test, or dropped ball. People give you that look. You start wondering if you have lost whatever made you good in the first place. The slump whispers, "Maybe this is who you really are."

Do not believe that lie. The slump is not your identity. It is your refining fire. Aaron Judge did not break a historic record in spite of his slump. He broke it through the slump. The struggle was always part of the story.

Keep swinging. Keep rising. Your record-breaking moment might be one single at-bat away, and all of heaven is already cheering you forward.

## Reflection:

Aaron Judge proved that slumps do not define you, they refine you. The willingness to keep stepping into the box is what separates champions from quitters. Where are you stuck in a slump right now, and what would it look like to keep swinging with faith instead of shrinking back?

## Prayer:

Lord, when I keep falling short, give me faith to rise again. My slump is not my story. My comeback is. Amen.

## Practice:

Write "Keep swinging" on your hand before your next competition. Every time doubt whispers, look at it and remember your breakthrough is coming.

# 6: CHARACTER — THE HEART WITHIN

# 31

# MIKE FISHER: THE MASKED INTEGRITY

"The integrity of the upright guides them, but the unfaithful are destroyed by their duplicity." - Proverbs 11:3

The arena roars so loud the ice seems to vibrate beneath Mike Fisher's skates. His Nashville Predators jersey is soaked in sweat. Two periods of brutal, physical NHL hockey are behind him, and his body aches from every check he absorbed along the boards. But what the cameras never capture is the moment right before the third period, when Mike quietly bows his head and whispers a prayer. Not for a goal. Not for a win. He prays for the strength to play with honor, no matter what happens next.

Mike Fisher built a legendary 17 season hockey career, and he did it without becoming someone he was ashamed of. In a sport where fighting earns standing ovations, Mike chose a different path. He competed fiercely, yes. He threw hard, clean hits. But he refused to let the culture of trash talk, cheap shots, and dirty retaliation define him. Teammates noticed. Opponents respected him. He earned the captain's "C" on his jersey not because he was the loudest voice in the locker room, but because he was the most consistent one.

Mike once said his faith was the foundation of everything. He looked at Proverbs 11:3 and understood that integrity is not a weakness. It is a compass. It does not make you soft. It makes you steady when everyone around you is crumbling under pressure. He realized that character is not what you show the crowd. Character is what you choose when nobody is filming.

Here is where this hits your life directly. Maybe you feel like being kind, honest, and fair does not get you anywhere. Maybe the kid who cuts corners or talks trash seems to win more attention. But attention is temporary. Character is permanent. When you choose integrity on the court, in the hallway, or in a group chat where someone is being torn apart, you are building something no scoreboard can measure. You are becoming someone people trust with real responsibility.

Being good does not mean being invisible. It means being unshakable. God sees every quiet act of honor you choose. Your integrity is your superpower. Wear it like armor under your jersey, and watch how it guides you through every challenge life throws your way.

## Reflection:

Mike Fisher proved that integrity makes you stronger, not weaker. True leadership is consistency in character, not volume. Do people trust you more for how you act when nobody is watching? What does your character say when the cameras are off?

## Prayer:

Lord, build integrity deep inside me. Help me choose what is right over what is easy, every single time. Amen.

## Practice:

Today, do one right thing nobody will see. Notice how it shapes your confidence from the inside out.

# 32

# TREVOR LAWRENCE: HUMILITY IN SPOTLIGHT

"Do nothing out of selfish ambition or vain conceit. Rather, in humility value others above yourselves." - Philippians 2:3

Trevor Lawrence steps up to the podium after leading Clemson to a National Championship, and the entire sports world is watching. He is only a freshman. Cameras flash in rapid bursts. Reporters scramble for quotes. ESPN analysts call him the best college quarterback prospect in a generation. But when the microphone reaches his lips, Trevor says something that stuns the room. He talks about his teammates. He credits his offensive line. He thanks God. He barely mentions himself.

Trevor Lawrence, the golden armed football quarterback with the unmistakable long hair, was handed every reason to become arrogant. He won a national title as a true freshman. He was projected as the number one NFL draft pick before his sophomore year even started. Magazine covers, highlight reels, and social media followers piled up around him like trophies. But Trevor treated all of it like borrowed equipment. He knew none of it belonged to him permanently.

In interviews, Trevor often shared that his identity was rooted in his faith, not his stats. He looked at Philippians 2:3 and saw a clear instruction. Christ himself chose to serve others rather than demand attention. If Jesus could wash feet, Trevor could deflect praise. He realized that real confidence does not need to announce itself. It simply shows up and does the work.

Think about your own week. Maybe you scored the winning basket or aced a test or led your group project. The temptation to soak in every compliment and replay your highlight reel is strong. But humility is not pretending you are bad at something. Humility is recognizing that your gifts come from God and they are meant to lift others, not just yourself. It means celebrating your teammate's assist as loudly as your own goal. It means thanking your coach instead of expecting applause.

When you stay humble under the spotlight, something incredible happens. People gravitate toward you. They trust you with bigger moments because they know success will not poison your heart. Arrogance builds walls. Humility builds teams. Let your talent speak, and let your character speak even louder. That is how champions with lasting legacies are truly made.

## Reflection:

Trevor Lawrence showed that humility is the ultimate form of strength, not weakness. Giving credit away actually multiplies your influence. When you succeed, do you spotlight yourself or your team? How can you practice deflecting praise this week?

## Prayer:

Father, keep my heart humble in every victory. Remind me that every gift I have flows from Your generous hand. Amen.

## Practice:

After your next win or achievement, publicly thank someone who helped you. Watch how it transforms the atmosphere around you.

# 33

# MANNY PACQUIAO: PRAYING FOR RIVALS

"Be devoted to one another in love. Honor one another above yourselves." – Romans 12:10

The lights in the MGM Grand Arena blaze white hot. Manny Pacquiao bounces lightly in his corner, rolling his shoulders, shaking out his fists. Across the ring stands a man trained to hurt him. In a few seconds, the bell will ring and violence will explode. But right now, in this sliver of silence, Manny does something almost no one in the building understands. He closes his eyes and prays for the man standing in the opposite corner.

Manny Pacquiao, the Filipino boxing legend and one of the most decorated fighters in history, carried a faith so deep it transformed how he viewed every opponent. He did not see an enemy across the ring. He saw another human being with a family, with fears, with a soul that God loved just as much as his own. Before brutal title fights that would leave both men bruised and bleeding, Manny would ask God to protect them both. He would ask for courage, fairness, and safety for his rival.

Manny lived Romans 12:10 in the most unlikely arena imaginable. He understood that honoring someone does not mean letting them win. It means recognizing their worth even in competition. He fought with everything he had once the bell rang. He threw devastating combinations and never backed down. But his heart never carried hatred into the ring. That distinction changed everything about his legacy.

Now picture your life. Maybe there is a rival on another team who frustrates you. Maybe a competitor beat you for a starting spot, and bitterness is growing like a weed in your chest. It feels natural to dislike them. It feels justified to wish for their failure. But here is the truth that separates ordinary athletes from extraordinary ones: your opponent is not your enemy. They are the person God placed in your path to sharpen you, challenge you, and reveal what is truly inside your heart.

When you choose to respect your rivals, even silently wishing them well before a game, you free yourself from the heavy weight of hate. Bitterness steals energy. Resentment clouds your focus. But a heart that honors others, even competitors, stays light, sharp, and ready. Pray for the person across the net, the field, or the court. It will not weaken your game. It will unleash the best version of you.

## Reflection:

Manny Pacquiao proved that fierce competition and genuine love for your opponent can exist together. Respect fuels greatness more than hatred ever could. Is there a rival you secretly resent? What would change inside you if you prayed for them before your next competition?

## Prayer:

God, replace any bitterness in my heart with genuine respect. Help me compete fiercely while honoring every opponent You place before me. Amen.

## Practice:

Before your next game, silently pray one kind sentence for your opponent. Notice how it shifts your focus and your peace.

# 34

# RUSSELL WILSON: STANDING AGAINST MOCKERY

"Blessed are you when people insult you, persecute you and falsely say all kinds of evil against you because of me." - Matthew 5:11

Russell Wilson walks into the Seattle Seahawks locker room the morning after a heartbreaking Super Bowl loss. The play call heard around the world, a last second interception on the goal line, replays on every screen in America. Reporters question his decisions. Social media tears him apart. But what stings differently is something quieter. Throughout his career, teammates, commentators, and critics have mocked Russell for being too vocal about his faith. They call him fake. They call him corny. They roll their eyes when he praises God after touchdowns.

Russell Wilson, the dynamic NFL quarterback with a rocket arm and lightning quick legs, has never hidden his Christianity. He speaks openly about Jesus in press conferences. He leads Bible studies. He publicly credits God with his success. And for all of it, he gets ridiculed. Not by strangers on the internet, but sometimes by people standing right next to him. In a league that celebrates aggression, Russell's gentle faith made him an easy target for mockery.

But Russell never flinched. He looked at Matthew 5:11 and found something surprising. Jesus did not say "if" people insult you for your faith. He said "when." That word changed Russell's entire perspective. Ridicule was not a sign that something was wrong. It was confirmation that he was standing for something real. He once said, "My faith is not a performance. It is the deepest truth about who I am."

You might feel this pressure right now. Maybe a teammate laughed when you bowed your head before a meal. Maybe a classmate mocked you for going to youth group instead of a party. That sting in your chest is real, and it is okay to feel it. But do not let it silence you. The people who mock conviction usually do so because it reveals something missing in their own lives. Your faith is not weakness. It is a bold declaration of who you belong to.

Stand tall. Speak kindly. Keep living out your beliefs through your actions. You do not need to argue or prove anything. Just keep showing up with the same quiet fire Russell carries onto every field. God honors the brave heart that refuses to hide, especially when the crowd makes it costly.

## Reflection:

Russell Wilson taught us that mockery for your faith is not a punishment. It is proof you are standing for something that matters deeply. When someone mocks your beliefs, do you shrink or stand firm? What gives you courage to keep living your faith publicly?

## Prayer:

Jesus, when they mock me, steady my heart. Give me courage to stand firm and grace to respond with love always. Amen.

## Practice:

This week, openly share one thing you believe in without apologizing. Notice who respects your courage and stands with you.

# 35

# MICHAEL PHELPS: REDEEMED FROM DARKNESS

"Though your sins are like scarlet, they shall be as white as snow; though they are red as crimson, they shall be like wool." - Isaiah 1:18

Michael Phelps stands on the pool deck at the 2016 Rio Olympics, water still streaming down his face, a gold medal hanging from his neck. Twenty three Olympic golds. The most decorated Olympian in human history. The crowd erupts. But behind his smile, Michael knows something the cameras never fully showed. Just two years earlier, he was sitting alone in a dark bedroom, so broken that he did not want to be alive.

Michael Phelps, the legendary American swimmer whose dominance in the pool rewrote every record book, nearly lost everything because of choices made outside the water. DUI arrests. Public scandals. A photograph that destroyed endorsements overnight. The world watched the golden boy crumble, and the headlines were ruthless. Michael felt like damaged goods, a cautionary tale wrapped in chlorine and shame. He believed his mistakes had permanently disqualified him from anything good.

Then a friend handed him Rick Warren's book, "The Purpose Driven Life." For the first time, Michael encountered a God who did not define people by their worst moments. He read Isaiah 1:18 and felt something crack open inside his chest. Scarlet sins washed white as snow. Not reduced. Not faded. Completely transformed. Michael wept. He began attending a Bible study group and slowly let faith rebuild the foundation his fame had shattered. He returned to the pool not chasing more gold but chasing purpose.

Maybe you are carrying something heavy right now. A mistake that replays in your mind on a loop. A moment you wish you could delete from your story. You look at other athletes, other students, and you think they have it together while you are permanently broken. That is a lie. Every single champion you admire has a chapter they almost did not survive. Your worst moment does not write your final page.

God is not waiting for you to become perfect before He accepts you. He meets you in the mess. He takes the stain and makes it vanish. Not because you earned it, but because His grace is that powerful. Michael Phelps walked into the darkest room of his life and found God already there, waiting with open arms. Your comeback story is not over. It is actually just beginning. Step into the light. You belong there.

## Reflection:

Michael Phelps proved that your darkest chapter does not define your destiny. God's grace transforms broken stories into powerful testimonies of redemption. What mistake are you letting define you? How would your confidence change if you truly believed God already forgave you completely?

## Prayer:

Father, wash my shame away and remind me that Your grace rewrites every broken chapter. My story is not over yet. Amen.

## Practice:

Write down one mistake you keep replaying. Then cross it out and write "forgiven" over it. Let that truth settle deep.

# 7: TEAMWORK & LEGACY — BEYOND YOURSELF

# 36

# MAYA MOORE: JUSTICE OVER TITLES

"He has shown you, O mortal, what is good. And what does the Lord require of you? To act justly and to love mercy and to walk humbly with your God." - Micah 6:8

Maya Moore stands at center court holding the WNBA championship trophy, golden confetti raining down on her Minnesota Lynx jersey. She has won four titles. She has two Finals MVP awards. She is the most dominant basketball player on the planet. The crowd roars her name. But behind her bright smile, something deeper is stirring inside her chest. A quiet voice whispers that her greatest victory has nothing to do with basketball.

In 2019, Maya shocked the entire sports world. She walked away from professional basketball at the peak of her career. Not because of injury. Not because of money. She stepped away to fight for the freedom of Jonathan Irons, a man wrongfully imprisoned for over two decades. Maya had met Jonathan through a prison ministry her family supported. She studied his case, hired attorneys, and poured her time, her energy, and her resources into pursuing justice. In 2020, Jonathan walked free. Maya gave up scoring titles to give a man his life back.

Maya looked at Micah 6:8 and realized that God never asked her to simply collect trophies. He asked her to act justly, to love mercy, and to walk humbly. She saw that her platform, her fame, and her talent were never just for her. They were tools God placed in her hands to serve something eternal.

Think about your own life for a second. You work so hard to win. You chase starting spots, MVP awards, and personal records. Those things matter. But what if God is preparing you for a purpose that stretches far beyond your sport? What if the discipline you are building right now is training you to fight for someone who cannot fight for themselves?

Winning is beautiful. But legacy is built when you use your influence to lift others. Maya proved that the bravest thing an athlete can do is not score the final basket. It is sacrifice comfort for someone else's freedom. You do not have to wait until you are famous. You can act justly at your school right now. Stand up for the kid who gets overlooked. Use your voice for those who feel invisible. That is the kind of championship that heaven celebrates.

## Reflection:

Maya Moore taught you that true greatness means using your gifts for justice and mercy, not just personal glory. God's scoreboard measures love. What matters more to you right now, winning for yourself or using your influence to help someone else? How could you start today?

## Prayer:

Lord, give me a heart for justice. Help me use my gifts to serve others and walk humbly with You always. Amen.

## Practice:

This week, find one person who feels invisible. Use your influence to encourage, include, or stand up for them.

# 37

# ALBERT PUJOLS: THE FAITHFUL SERVANT

"His master replied, 'Well done, good and faithful servant! You have been faithful with a few things; I will put you in charge of many things.'" - Matthew 25:21

Albert Pujols tips his batting helmet toward the roaring crowd in St. Louis on a warm summer night. The crack of his bat still echoes through Busch Stadium. Over 700 career home runs. Three MVP awards. Two World Series rings. The man they call "The Machine" has crushed baseballs for over two decades. But as his final season winds down, Albert is not thinking about his stats. He is thinking about something that will outlast every single number on his baseball card.

Albert grew up in the Dominican Republic with very little. When he gave his life to Jesus as a young man, everything shifted. He did not suddenly become a better hitter. He became a more faithful person. Albert and his wife Deidre started the Pujols Family Foundation, serving families affected by Down syndrome and providing support for the poor in the Dominican Republic. Albert treated every at-bat as an offering to God. He played with the same intensity in April as he did in October. He showed up early. He stayed late. He never cut corners, even when no one was watching.

Albert read Matthew 25:21 and understood that God was not going to ask him how many home runs he hit. God was going to ask if he was faithful with the gifts he received. Faithful in the big moments, yes. But also faithful in the boring Tuesday practices, the long road trips, and the painful rehab sessions.

Here is what this means for you. Someday your season will end. Your jersey will hang in a closet. The question will not be how many points you scored. The question will be: were you faithful? Did you give your best effort when no one clapped? Did you encourage your teammate when you were frustrated? Did you honor God with the small, invisible moments of your day?

Faithfulness is not flashy. It is showing up, doing the work, and trusting that God sees every quiet sacrifice. Albert's legacy is not just 700 home runs. It is thousands of lives changed through consistent, humble obedience. You are building that same kind of legacy right now, one faithful choice at a time.

## Reflection:

Albert Pujols showed you that lasting legacy comes from faithfulness, not fame. God rewards those who honor Him in the unseen moments. Are you being faithful with what God has already given you, your time, your talent, your attitude? Where can you be more consistent?

## Prayer:

Father, help me be faithful in small things. I want to hear "well done" from You above all. Amen.

## Practice:

Pick one responsibility you have been lazy about this week. Commit to doing it with excellence today, as an offering to God.

# 38

# DEREK CARR: LEADING THE LOCKER

"Though one may be overpowered, two can defend themselves. A cord of three strands is not quickly broken." - Ecclesiastes 4:9-12

Derek Carr jogs off the field after a brutal loss. His Las Vegas Raiders teammates sit scattered across the locker room with their heads down. Some slam helmets into lockers. Others stare at the floor in silence. The frustration is thick and heavy. But Derek, the team's quarterback and outspoken follower of Christ, does something unexpected. He walks to the center of the room and speaks. Not about the missed plays. Not about blame. He talks about brotherhood. He asks his teammates to lock arms and pray.

Derek grew up in Bakersfield, California, in a family that loved football and loved Jesus. When he entered the NFL, he quickly noticed that locker room culture could be brutal. Gossip, selfishness, and finger-pointing could destroy a team faster than any opponent. Derek decided he would not just lead on the field. He would lead in the spaces no camera could see. He started Bible studies. He invited teammates to his home. He checked in on rookies who felt lost and overwhelmed.

Derek looked at Ecclesiastes 4:9-12 and saw that God designed strength to be shared. A single thread snaps easily, but cords woven together hold strong under pressure. He realized that real leadership is not about having the loudest voice. It is about creating an environment where people feel safe enough to grow.

Now think about your team. Maybe the culture is rough. Maybe people gossip, tear each other down, or only care about themselves. You might feel powerless to change it. But Derek Carr proved that one person who chooses encouragement over criticism can shift the entire atmosphere. You do not need a captain's title to lead. You need a servant's heart.

Start small. Sit with the teammate who always eats alone. Speak up when someone gets mocked behind their back. Organize a group that holds each other accountable. Culture changes one conversation at a time. When you weave faith into the fabric of your team, you create something that no scoreboard can measure. You build a cord of three strands. You build the kind of team that the enemy cannot break.

## Reflection:

Derek Carr showed you that one voice rooted in faith can transform a toxic team culture into something unbreakable. Leadership starts with love. What is one thing about your team's culture that bothers you? What small step could you take this week to begin changing it?

## Prayer:

God, give me courage to lead with love. Help me build unity and point my teammates toward Your strength. Amen.

## Practice:

This week, encourage one teammate privately. Send a text, say something kind after practice, or invite someone new to sit with you.

# 39

# ABBY WAMBACH: PASSING THE TORCH

"Whoever wants to become great among you must be your servant, and whoever wants to be first must be slave of all." - Mark 10:43-45

Abby Wambach stands on the pitch after her final international soccer match, surrounded by red, white, and blue confetti. The crowd screams her name. She has scored 184 goals for the United States Women's National Team, more than any player in international history. Tears stream down her face. But in this golden moment, Abby does not clutch the spotlight for herself. She turns, finds her younger teammates, and wraps them in her arms. She whispers words of belief into their ears. She is handing them the torch.

Abby grew up in Rochester, New York, the youngest of seven children in a competitive, faith-filled family. She learned early that greatness is never just about what you accomplish. It is about what you leave behind. Throughout her career, Abby was known for lifting up the players around her. She celebrated their goals louder than her own. She mentored young athletes who were terrified of failing on the world stage. She understood that her job was not only to score but to prepare the next generation to carry the mission forward.

Abby lived the truth of Mark 10:43-45. Jesus never told His followers to climb to the top and stay there. He said the greatest among you serves everyone else. Abby realized that the most powerful thing she could do with her platform was not hold onto it. It was to give it away.

This is where it gets personal for you. Maybe you are the oldest on your team or the most experienced player. Maybe you have a few years left before your final game. The question is not just what records you will set. The question is: who are you pouring into? Legacy is not a trophy in a case. Legacy is a younger athlete who plays with more confidence because you believed in them first.

Start now. Pull a younger player aside and tell them what you see in them. Share what you have learned through your failures, not just your wins. When you serve the people coming after you, your impact multiplies beyond anything you could achieve alone. The torch is already in your hands. The bravest thing you will ever do is pass it on.

## Reflection:

Abby Wambach proved that true greatness is measured by what you pour into others, not what you keep for yourself. Legacy lives in people. Who is a younger or less experienced person you could encourage and invest in this week? What would you say to them?

## Prayer:

Lord, teach me to serve and invest in others. Help me build a legacy that outlasts my final game. Amen.

## Practice:

Find a younger athlete or teammate this week. Share one lesson you have learned and speak genuine encouragement over their future.

# 40

# MATT DUCHENE: IRON SHARPENS IRON

"As iron sharpens iron, so one person sharpens another." – Proverbs 27:17

Matt Duchene glides across the ice under the bright lights of Bridgestone Arena, his Nashville Predators jersey cutting through the cold air. The puck dances on his stick. The crowd is electric. Matt has played over 1,000 NHL hockey games. He has represented Canada on the world stage. He has scored highlight-reel goals that live forever on replay. But ask Matt what fuels him most, and he will not mention the goals. He will talk about the men who sharpen his faith every single day.

Matt grew up in Haliburton, Ontario, where hockey and church were woven into the rhythm of his childhood. When he entered the NHL as a young player, he quickly felt the loneliness that comes with being a Christian in a locker room full of different lifestyles. The travel, the late nights, and the pressure made it easy to drift spiritually. Then Matt discovered Hockey Ministries International and connected with other players who shared his faith. He joined Bible studies with teammates and chapel services before games. Suddenly, he was not carrying his belief alone. He had brothers who challenged him, held him accountable, and prayed with him through the hardest seasons.

Matt clung to Proverbs 27:17 like a lifeline. He realized that faith was never meant to be a solo sport. Iron does not sharpen itself. You need someone strong enough to push against you, challenge your thinking, and call out the greatness God placed inside you. Matt found that his game improved when his faith community grew stronger. The two were deeply connected.

Maybe right now you feel alone in your faith. Maybe your teammates do not share your beliefs. Maybe you feel weird praying before a game or reading your Bible in the locker room. Hear this clearly: you are not weird. You are brave. But you also need people who sharpen you. Find one person, a teammate, a friend, a coach, a mentor, who will walk with you spiritually. Start a conversation about faith. Join a group. You were never meant to fight your battles by yourself.

When iron meets iron, sparks fly. That friction is not a problem. It is the process that makes you sharper, stronger, and more prepared for everything ahead. Find your iron. Let God use that friendship to forge you into something unstoppable.

## Reflection:

Matt Duchene showed you that faith grows stronger in community, not isolation. You need people who challenge and sharpen your walk with God. Do you have someone in your life who sharpens your faith? If not, who could you reach out to and start that journey with?

## Prayer:

Father, lead me to friends who sharpen my faith. Give me boldness to seek community and never walk alone. Amen.

## Practice:

This week, reach out to one person and start a faith conversation. Invite them to pray, read Scripture, or simply talk honestly.

# FINAL WHISTLE

You just finished forty stories of real athletes who trusted God through the fire and came out stronger on the other side. Take a breath and let that sink in. You walked with Manny Pacquiao through the quiet discipline of early mornings. You stood with Maya Moore as she traded championships for justice. You watched Albert Pujols play his final game with faithfulness that outlasted every home run. You felt the Christ-centered courage of Derek Carr transforming a broken locker room. These were not fairy tales. These were Christ followers who decided that God's plan was bigger than any scoreboard.

Every chapter carried a thread that ties directly to your life right now. You learned that confidence is not something you fake. It is something you forge through daily habits, Christ-centered identity, and relentless faithfulness. You discovered that setbacks are not the end of your story. They are the Christ-shaped turning points that build the resilience and character the world desperately needs. You saw that teamwork, legacy, and serving others matter more than personal glory. And most importantly, you realized that God is not sitting in the stands watching from a distance. He is right beside you in the huddle, whispering purpose into every practice, every prayer, and every painful moment of growth.

But here is the truth that separates readers from game changers. Knowledge without action stays stuck on the page. So do not let these stories collect dust in your memory. Live them out. Set a goal this week. Build a system tonight. Encourage a teammate tomorrow. Stand up for someone who feels invisible. Pray before you perform. These small, faithful choices are what forge exceptional character over time.

To help you stay accountable, I have created an Advent-style accountability calendar designed to walk you through daily action steps that match the lessons in this book. It will keep you consistent, focused, and faith-fueled long after you close this final page.

And if these stories lit something inside your heart and you want more Christ-centered content to keep growing, search for Cyrus

Ellison online or find any of my books and click the author name. There is so much more waiting for you.

You are not just a teen who read a book. You are a God-equipped, purpose-driven game changer. The unshakable confidence, the crushed goals, the exceptional character you read about in these pages? That is your story now. Go write it.

You got this. And more importantly, God's got you.

# A TRUE BLESSING!

If this book has encouraged you or helped you feel less alone, would you leave a quick review?

Even one sentence makes a huge difference and takes just a minute. As a small author, your feedback not only lifts my heart... it also helps other women of faith with find the support and hope they need.

Thank you for being part of this journey!

Scan this QR code with your phone to go to the review page and find this book.

Or

Go to your orders, find the book and click

"Write a product review"

Thank you <3